东方智慧丛书

The Wisdom of the East Series

The Wisdom of the East Series

东方智慧丛书

Editors-in-Chief: Tang Wenhui　Liu Zhiqiang

主编：汤文辉　刘志强

Academic Adviser: Zhang Baoquan

学术顾问：张葆全

Chinese-English

汉　英　对　照

Higher Education and *The Universal Order* (Selections)

大学中庸选译

Compiled and Commented by Zhang Baoquan

选释：张葆全

Translated by Gu Hongming　Wu Siyuan

翻译：辜鸿铭　吴思远

Illustrated by Zheng Zhenming　Lan Xuehui

绘图：郑振铭　蓝学会

· 桂林 Gui Lin ·

GUANGXI NORMAL UNIVERSITY PRESS

广西师范大学出版社

图书在版编目（CIP）数据

大学中庸选译：汉英对照 / 张葆全选释；辜鸿铭，吴思远译；郑振铭，蓝学会绘．—桂林：广西师范大学出版社，2016.8
（东方智慧丛书 / 汤文辉等主编）
ISBN 978-7-5495-8502-1

Ⅰ．①大… Ⅱ．①张…②辜…③吴…④郑…⑤蓝… Ⅲ．①儒家②《大学》－译文－汉、英③《中庸》－译文－汉、英 Ⅳ．①B222.14

中国版本图书馆 CIP 数据核字（2016）第 162201 号

广西师范大学出版社出版发行
（广西桂林市中华路 22 号　邮政编码：541001
网址：http://www.bbtpress.com）
出版人：张艺兵
全国新华书店经销
广西大华印刷有限公司印刷
（广西南宁市高新区科园大道 62 号　邮政编码：530007）
开本：880 mm × 1 240 mm　1/32
印张：11.375　　字数：230 千字　　图：50 幅
2016 年 8 月第 1 版　　2016 年 8 月第 1 次印刷
定价：86.00 元

总 序

文化交流对人类社会的存在与发展至关重要。季羡林先生曾指出，文化交流是推动人类社会前进的主要动力之一，文化一旦产生，就必然交流，这种交流是任何力量也阻挡不住的。由于文化交流，世界各民族的文化才能互相补充，共同发展，才能形成今天世界上万紫千红的文化繁荣现象。[1]

中国与东盟国家的文化交流亦然，并且具有得天独厚的优势。首先，中国与东盟许多国家地理相接，山水相连，不少民族之间普遍存在着跨居、通婚现象，这为文化交流奠定了良好的地理与人文基础。其次，古代中国与世界其他国家建立起的“海上丝绸之路”为中国与东盟国家的经济、文化交流创造了有利的交通条件。

中国与东盟诸多使用不同语言文字的民族进行思想与文化对话，自然离不开翻译。翻译活动一般又分为口译和笔译两类。有史记载的

[1]季羡林：《文化的冲突与融合·序》，载张岱年、汤一介等《文化的冲突与融合》，北京大学出版社，1997年，第2页。

中国与东盟之间的口译活动可以追溯至西周时期，但笔译活动则出现在明代，至今已逾五百年的历史。

在过去五百年的历史长河中，东盟国家大量地译介了中国的文化作品，其中不少已经融入到本国的文化中去。中国译介东盟国家的作品也不在少数。以文字为载体的相互译介活动，更利于文化的传承与发展，把中国与东盟国家的文化交流推上了更高的层次。

2013 年 9 月，国务院总理李克强在广西南宁举行的第十届中国—东盟博览会开幕式上发表主旨演讲时指出，中国与东盟携手开创了合作的“黄金十年”。他呼吁中国与东盟百尺竿头更进一步，创造新的“钻石十年”。2013 年 10 月，习近平总书记在周边外交工作座谈会上强调要对外介绍好我国的内外方针政策，讲好中国故事，传播好中国声音，把中国梦同周边各国人民过上美好生活的愿望、同地区发展前景对接起来，让命运共同体意识在周边国家落地生根。于是，把中华文化的经典译介至东盟国家，不仅具有重要的历史意义，同时还蕴含着浓厚的时代气息。

所谓交流，自然包括“迎来送往”，《礼记》有言：“往而不来，非礼也；来而不往，亦非礼也。”中国与东盟国家一样，既翻译和引进外国的优秀文化，同时也把本国文化的精髓部分推介出去。作为中国最具人文思想的出版社之一——广西师范大学出版社构想了《东方智慧丛书》，并付诸实践，不仅是中国翻译学界、人文学界的大事，更是中国与东盟进行良好沟通、增进相互了解的必然选择。广东外语外贸大学和广西民族大学作为翻译工作的主要承担方，都是国家外语非通用语种本科人才培养基地，拥有东盟语言文字的翻译优势。三个单位的合作将能够擦出更多的火花，向东盟国家更好地传播中华文化。

联合国教科文组织的官员认为，“文化交流是新的全球化现象”。[1]我们希望顺应这一历史潮流与时代趋势，做一点力所能及的事。

是为序。

刘志强

2015 年 1 月 25 日

[1]《联合国教科文组织文化政策与跨文化对话司司长卡特瑞娜·斯泰诺的致辞》，载《世界文化的东亚视角》，北京大学出版社，2004年，第3页。

Preface to The Wisdom of the East Series

Cultural exchanges are of significant importance to the existence and development of human society. Mr. Ji Xianlin once pointed out that cultural exchange was one of the major driving forces for the progress of human society. It is inevitable that communications and exchanges will occur among different cultures. As a result, the interaction and mutual enrichment of cultures contribute to the formation of a diversified world featured by cultural prosperity.[1]

The cultural exchange between China and ASEAN countries, in the trend of mutual communication and interaction, also boasts of its own unique strengths. First of all, China borders many ASEAN countries both by land and by sea, and intermarriage and transnational settlement are common, all of which lay a solid foundation for cultural exchanges. In addition, the "Maritime Silk

[1] Ji Xianlin, "Preface to Cultural Conflicts and Integration", in *Cultural Conflicts and Integration*, edited by Zhang Dainian, Tang Yijie, et al. Beijing: Beijing University Press, 1997, p.2.

Road" developed by ancient China and other countries has helped pave the way to a smooth economic and cultural exchange between China and ASEAN countries.

People from China and ASEAN countries use different languages. Thus, to conduct a successful dialogue in the cultural field requires the involvement of translation and oral interpretation. Historical records show that the oral interpretation among people of China and ASEAN can be dated back to the Western Zhou Dynasty (1122-771 B.C.). It is also known that translation started to boom in the Ming Dynasty, which was five hundred years ago.

In the past five hundred years, a large number of Chinese cultural works were translated into many languages of ASEAN countries and many of which have been integrated into their local cultures. China has also translated a lot of works of ASEAN countries. Translation is beneficial to inheritance and development of culture and upgrades the cultural exchanges between China and ASEAN to a higher level.

As Mr. Li Keqiang, Premier of the State Council of the People's Republic of China, pointed out in his speech at the opening ceremony of the 10th China-ASEAN Expo held in Nanning in September, 2013, China and ASEAN jointly created "10 golden years" of cooperation. And he called on both sides to upgrade their cooperation to a new level by creating "10 diamond years". In October, 2013, General Secretary Xi Jinping emphasized, in a meeting with Chinese diplomats, the importance of introducing China's domestic and foreign policies to other countries and regions, and making Chinese voice heard in the world. Xi also pointed out that "China Dream" should be connected with her neighboring countries' dream of a better life and with the development prospect of those countries so as to build up a community of shared destiny. Against such a backdrop, it's of both historical and current significance to translate Chinese classics and introduce them to ASEAN countries.

Exchanges are reciprocal. According to the *Book of Rites*, behaviors that do not reciprocate are not consistent with rites. Like ASEAN countries, China has had excellent foreign cultural works translated and introduced domestically, and also translate and introduce to the outside world the essence of local culture and thoughts. Guangxi Normal University Press, one of the top presses in China that focus on enhancing the influence of the humanities, made the decision to publish *The Wisdom of the East Series*. It is not only a big event in Chinese academia, but also a necessary choice for China and ASEAN to communicate with each other and enhance mutual understanding. Guangxi University for Nationalities, and Guangdong University of Foreign Studies, the main undertakers of the translation project, are both national non-universal languages training bases for undergraduates and boasts strengths of ASEAN languages. Cooperation between the two universities and the press will surely facilitate dissemination of traditional Chinese culture to ASEAN countries.

UNESCO officials hold the belief that cultural exchange is a new phenomenon of globalization.[1] We hope that our efforts could breathe the spirit of this historical momentum and help ASEAN countries understand Chinese culture better.

Liu Zhiqiang

January 25, 2015

---

[1] "Speech of Katerina stenou, Director of Division of Cultural Policies and Intercultural Dialogue", from *East Asia's View on World Culture*. Beijing: Beijing University Press, 2004, p.3.

前　言

《大学》和《中庸》，原为《礼记》中的两篇。南宋朱熹把《大学》和《中庸》与《论语》、《孟子》编在一起，称为“四书”，供读书人阅读。朱熹还撰写了《四书章句集注》（含《大学章句》、《中庸章句》、《论语集注》、《孟子集注》），解释了“四书”的文字和义理。在编辑时，朱熹对《大学》和《中庸》原文进行了分章，对《大学》的文字还做了一些调整。

由于南宋以后，历代科举考试主要考“四书”“五经”，所以“四书”“五经”成为读书人必读的“教科书”。“四书”“五经”的思想，日益深入人心，对古代中国人（尤其是知识分子）世界观、人生观的形成，产生了非常巨大的影响。其中包含着许多极为优秀的思想文化传统，值得我们继承和发扬。

《大学》——为学修身之正途

今天，《大学》对于我们，可以看作是：教育之纲领，为学之正途，修身之极则，从政之宝典。

朱熹说：“大，过去读音读成泰，今天读音仍读成大。”在春秋末年孔子创办私学之前，“学在官府”（学校都是官办的），大学即国家的最高学府。《礼记·王制》说：“小学设在宫廷的左侧，大学设在城郊。天子设立的大学叫辟雍，诸侯设立的大学叫泮宫。”《大戴礼记·保傅》说：“古时候，小孩八岁时就开始上小学，学习基础的文化技艺，练习基本的礼节，培养初步的道德情操。十五岁就上大学，学习较为精深的文化技艺，练习较为繁复的礼节，按成人要求培养高尚的道德情操。”东汉郑玄在《礼记目录》中说：“在大学里，学子们广博地学习（学做人的道理，学从政的才能），可以为以后从政打下基础。”

在《大学章句》中，朱熹引程颐之言说：“《大学》是孔子儒家学派传世的典籍，是初学者学习精研道德学问的入门书。在今天要了解古人怎样学习精研道德学问，就靠这部《大学》，其次则是《论语》和《孟子》。”他告诉我们，古人求学，《大学》是必须首先研读的。

朱熹将《大学》分为 11 章，说：“第一章是经，是孔子说的话，是孔子弟子曾子记录下来的；后面十章是传（按：第五章为朱熹所补），是曾子的解释，是他的弟子门人记录下来的。”

曾子即曾参（前 505—前 435），字子舆，鲁国武城人，孔子弟子，《史记·仲尼弟子列传》说他小孔子 46 岁。其父曾点，也是孔子弟子。据《论语》记载，曾参严于律己，说“我每天都要多次反省我自己”。认为年轻学子“应把施行仁德于天下作为自己的使命”，因而年轻学子必定是“负担沉重而路途遥远”。他事亲至孝，并特别看重“孝”道，认为“在上位的人如果能恭谨地对待父母的死亡，追念而不忘祖先的功绩，老百姓的道德风气也就会跟着归于淳朴忠厚”。《史记·仲尼弟子列传》说："孔子认为他精通孝道，所以对他进行了特别的传授。后来他写了《孝经》。"曾子也曾收徒讲学，孔子之孙子思是他的弟子，而孟子又敬仰子思，拜子思门人为师。由于曾子之传授而形成的"思孟学派"，成为儒家的正统学派。《汉书·艺文志》著录《曾子》十八篇，早已亡佚，今仅《孝经》、《大学》传世。此外，在《大戴礼记》、《孔子家语》等书中，有一些曾子言行的记载。

《中庸》——为人处世之宝典

中庸哲学是孔子的认识论，是他认识事物、处理矛盾的思想方法，也是他为人处世的道德标准。中庸哲学体现了孔子解决一切理论和实践问题的最高智慧。从《论语》、《孟子》等书来看，孔子的中庸思想，有"执中守正"、"折中致和"、"因时制宜通权达变"等含义。

东汉郑玄在《礼记目录》中谈到《中庸》篇时说："它的名称叫作'中庸'，是因为它所阐述的是'中和'的践行和功用。'庸'的意思就是'用'。"

朱熹在《中庸章句》开头解题时说："'中'，是不偏不倚、无过不及的名称。'庸'，是'平常'的意思。程子说：'不偏就叫作中，不易就叫作庸。中是天下的正道，庸是天下的定理。'"由此可知，孔孟儒家所说的中庸，就是恪守中道，坚持原则，不偏不倚，从容适度，不走极端，无"过"无"不及"。在处理矛盾时善于执两用中，协调致和，追求中正、中和、稳定、和谐。并且随时以处中，因时制宜，与时俱进。

中庸哲学所说的"中"，本身就包含了"和"。儒家文化讲"和而不同"（协调致和而不强行同一），讲"和实生物，同则不继"（阴阳协调从而致和就能滋生繁衍万物，强行同一万物就不能持续繁衍），其实质就是重视差异，尊重他人，尊重不同意见，重视协调，折中致和，崇尚和谐。

中庸之道，是儒家坚定的信仰和追求。儒家视中庸之道为"修身"

之极则，也是“治国平天下”的正道。

朱熹将《中庸》分为33章，并按全文内容，提示其论述要点。按照提示，全文可分为三个部分：第一部分，1—11章，重点论“中庸”，说明“执中守正是天下一切情感和道理的根本；折中致和，是天下一切事物的普遍原则。达到‘中和’的境界，天地便各在其位了，万物便生长繁育了”，中庸之道是“不可以片刻离开”的。第二部分，12—20章，重点论“道”，说明“中庸之道并不是远离人们的”，中庸之道的运用，既广大又精微。第三部分，21—33章，重点论“诚”，说明“诚”既是“天之道”，也是“人之道”。《中庸》论“诚”，实际上是论人的信仰和追求，也就是对中庸之道的信仰和追求。

朱熹说：“此篇是孔子儒家所传授的‘心法’（代代传授最为重要的心得和方法），子思恐怕时间久远而走样失真，所以用笔写了下来，后来他的门人便传授给孟子。”

《史记·孔子世家》记载，子思（前483－前402），名孔伋，字子思，孔鲤（字伯鱼）之子，孔子之孙，作《中庸》。《史记·孟子荀卿列传》说，孟子曾受业于子思之门人。《汉书·艺文志》著录《子思》二十三篇，早已亡佚，今仅《中庸》、《表记》、《坊记》（均收入《礼记》中）传世。但今本《中庸》有的文字，如二十八章“今天下车同轨，书同文，行同伦”等语，明显为秦汉间人所增补。

朱熹对《中庸》一书极为推崇，说：“这部书开头只说中庸一理，中间扩散发挥涉及万事万物，最后又归结为中庸一理。放开去它充满在天地东南西北各方，收起来可珍藏于密室之中。它的意味无穷无尽，都是实实在在的学问。善于读书的人认真研读玩味就会有莫大的收获，终身运用它就会感受到它的功用无穷无尽。”

本书从《大学》和《中庸》中精选了100条进行译解，原文均据朱熹《四书章句集注》（中华书局 2011 年 1 月出版），各条标题，为中文译解者据原文和朱熹解说所加。中文译解者对原文进行了通俗易懂的翻译和解析，力求将《大学》、《中庸》思想的原貌及其精髓较为完整地呈现在读者面前。希望《大学》、《中庸》的思想精华，能给今天的人们以及子孙后代带来更多的有益启示。

Foreword

The texts of *Daxue* [Higher Education] and *Zhongyong* [The Universal Order] are originally from *Liji* [Book of Rituals]. A Southern Song philosopher Zhu Xi (1130—1200) compiled the "Four Books," namely, *Lunyu* [Analects], *Mengzi* [Mencius], *Daxue* and *Zhongyong*. Zhu also wrote the *Sishu zhangju jizhu* [The Annotated Four Books] (namely *Daxue zhangju*, *Zhongyong zhangju*, *Lunyu jizhu* and *Mengzi jizhu*) in order to provide his glossarial annotations and textual exegeses. He divided the texts of *Daxue* and *Zhongyong* into chapters and made some verbal changes for the latter.

From the Southern Song on, imperial examinations in each following dynasty mainly focused on the "Four Books" and the "Five Canons." Therefore, these Confucian classics have become the standard textbooks for ancient Chinese scholars and students alike. The principles and thoughts of Confucianism were deeply entrenched in the minds of ancient Chinese, particularly the intellectuals, and exerted a tremendous influence in forming their outlook on world and life. This excellent ideological and cultural tradition deserves to be inherited and carried forward by later generations.

Daxue, or *Higher Education* —The Right Path to Education and Self-Cultivation

Today, *Daxue* could still be regarded as the guidelines of education, the right path to scholarship, the regulations for self-cultivation and the treasured canon for people in authority.

Zhu Xi once commented, "The character '*da*,' or translated as 'higher,' 'great,' was pronounced '*tai*'." Before Confucius established his private schools in the late years of Spring and Autumn Period, "there were only government-run schools," and *daxue*, or Higher Education Academy, was the institute of learning at the highest level. According to one chapter entitled "Imperial Systems and Regulations" found in *Liji*, "the National Academy for Primary Education was set up on the left side of the imperial palace, and the Higher Education Academy in the suburbs. The *daxue* founded by the emperor was called *piyong*, and that by the dukes and princes was called *pangong*." It can also be found in the chapter "Educational Advisers" in *Da Dai Liji* [*Book of Rituals* by Dai De] that "in ancient times, a boy at age of eight would attend the National Academy for Primary Education to learn basic knowledge and skills, to practice simple rituals and to cultivate moral character. At age of fifteen, he would attend the Higher Education Academy to study profound knowledge and advanced skills, to practice sophisticated rituals, and to improve moral character according to the requirements of moral integrity for an adult." Zheng Xuan (127—200) of Eastern Han dynasty recorded in *Liji mulu* [*The Catalogue of Book of Rituals*] that "scholars at the Higher Education Academy studies so extensively that they lay a solid foundation for their future political career."

In his *Daxue Zhangju* [The Annotated *Daxue*], Zhu Xi quoted Cheng Yi (1033—1107) and said, "*Daxue* is a Confucian classic handed down from scholars in ancient times, and it is a primer for beginners who aim to study morality. That we are now able see how the ancient scholars studied morality is solely owning to the preservation of this work. *Lunyu* and *Mengzi* come after it."

Zhu Xi divided *Daxue* into eleven chapters and explained, "The first chapter can be taken as the canon, for it contains quotations from Confucius and was recorded by his disciple Zengzi; the following ten chapters (Note: the fifth chapter was by Zhu Xi) were about the exegesis by Zengzi, which were recorded by Zeng's disciples."

Zengzi, whose name was actually Zeng Shen (505—435 B.C.) and literary name Ziyu, came from City Wu of Lu State. He was one of Confucius' disciples. It was recorded in *Shiji* [Historical Documents] that Zeng was forty-six years younger than his teacher and his father Zeng Dian also studied with Confucius. According to *Lunyu*, Zeng Shen exercised strict self-discipline, and he said "I reflect on myself several times a day." He thought that young scholars "should take the cause of furthering humanity and morality in the world as their own mission." Therefore, they are bound to "bear heavy burdens on a long road." Zeng attached great importance to filial piety, and he maintained that "the moral standards of the general public will be improved and the ethos of the whole society purified, if men in authority are able to treat respectfully and cautiously the death of their parents, and treasure the merits of their ancestors." His biographical accounts in *Shiji* show that "Confucius thought Zeng understood the values of filial piety, so he passed all he knew about the filial piety to Zeng in his teaching. Later, Zeng wrote *Xiaojing* [Book of Filial Piety]." Zeng also had many students, and Zisi, the grandson of Confucius, was one of them. Moreover, Mencius thought very highly of Zeng, and he studied with one of Zeng's students. Thus the "School of Zisi and Mencius" had become the orthodoxy in Confucianism. In *Hanshu* [Book of Han], it has been recorded that there were eighteen chapters in the book *Zengzi*, yet the book was lost, and to date, only *Xiaojing* and *Daxue* exist. There are some sketchy accounts of Zengzi found in books such as *Da Dai Liji*, *Kongzi jiayu*, etc.

Zhongyong, or *The Universal Order* —The Treasured Canon for Human Conducts

The philosophical thoughts in *Zhongyong* are Confucius' understanding of all matters in the world, his solutions to the common problems, and the moral standards for conducts of life. The book is indicative of the highest wisdom of Confucius in his dealing with both theoretical and practical issues. Compared with *Lunyu* and *Mengzi*, *Zhongyong* concentrates more on the ideas such as "maintaining the central point and guarding the upright," "keeping the central balance and fulfilling the moral sense," and "acting according to the changing circumstances" etc.

Zheng Xuan discussed about *Zhongyong* in *Liji mulu*, and he said, "The book was entitled '*Zhongyong*,' because it is mainly concerned with the practice and application of 'central harmony,' or "true moral being and moral order." '*Yong*' means 'to use, practice and apply.'"

Zhu Xi explained in the beginning of his *Zhongyong zhangju* that "'*zhong*' is the name for what is without inclination or deflection, which neither exceeds nor comes short. '*Yong*' means ordinary, constant. The master, the philosopher Cheng, says: 'Being without inclination to either side is called *zhong*; admitting of no change is called *yong*.' By *zhong* is denoted the correct course to be pursued by all under heaven; by *yong* is denoted the fixed principle regulating all under heaven." These words from the Confucian school are to warn people against going to extremes, for one must scrupulously and impartially observe the moral order in one's thinking and action, taking the appropriate measure at a sedate pace. It is wrong "to go beyond the mark," or "not to come up to it." In dealing with a problem, we need to take the two extremes of negative and positive, and apply the mean of the two extremes. We need to adopt the "mean measures" in accordance with the "moral order." This is what is called "maintaining the central point and guarding the upright," or "keeping the central balance and fulfilling the moral sense." It is important to act according to circumstances and advance with times.

"*Zhong*," or "central point, central balance," embodies the wisdom of "*he*," or "agreement, harmony." According to Confucianism, "a moral man is social but not familiar" (He agrees but does not always echo), and "balance and harmony lead to development, but sameness impedes continuation." In essence, Confucianists treasure diversity, different opinions from other people, balance and harmony.

The Confucian scholars believe in and unswervingly pursue the universal moral order, for it is the ultimate regulation for "self-cultivation" and right path to "secure a good government and further the cause of enlightenment and civilization in the world."

Additionally, Zhu divided *Zhongyong* into thirty three chapters and he also provided his comments and summaries. There can be, according to Zhu's annotations, three major parts: the first part consists of the first eleven chapters, and it focuses on "the universal moral order." "Our true self or moral being is the great reality existence, and moral order is the universal law in the world." "When true moral being and moral order are realized, the universe then becomes a cosmos and all things attain their full growth and development." Hence, "The moral law is a law from whose operation we cannot for one instant in our existence escape." Chapters from twelve to twenty form the second part in which "moral law" was elaborated. "The moral law is not something away from the actuality of human life." It is universally applicable, and it functions both extensively and minutely. The third part contains the rest chapters, and is mainly concerned with "absolute truth." "Truth is the law of God. Acquired truth is the law of man." The discussion on "truth," as a matter of fact, aims to emphasize on what human beings should believe in and pursue: the universal moral order.

Zhu Xi commented, "This work contains the law of the mind, which was handed down from one to another, in the Confucian school, till Zisi, fearing lest in the course of time errors should arise about it, committed it to writing, and delivered it to Mencius."

According to the biographical accounts in *Shiji*, the name of Zisi (483—402 B.C.) is Kong Ji and his literary name is Zisi. As the author of *Zhongyong*, he was also the son of Kong Li (literary name Boyu) and the grandson of Confucius. It was recorded that Mencius once studied with one of Zisi's students. The book title *Zisi* was recorded in *Hanshu*, yet the twenty three chapters in the book were lost for a long time. Today only *Zhongyong*, *Biaoji* and *Fangji* (the three were all collected in *Liji*) survive. But it is easy to tell that some of the texts in *Zhongyong* were added by later scholars during the Qin and Han Dynasties, such as the sentence "Now under the heaven carriages have all wheels of the same size; all writing is with the same characters; and all conduct there are the same rules" found in chapter twenty eight.

Zhu Xi spoke very highly of *Zhongyong*: "The book first speaks of one principle; it next spreads this out, and embraces all things; finally, it returns and gathers them all up under the one principle. Unroll it, and it fills the universe; roll it up, and it retires and lies hid in mysteriousness. The relish of it is inexhaustible. The whole of it is solid learning. When the skilful reader has explored it with delight till he has apprehended it, he may carry it into practice all his life, and will find that it cannot be exhausted."

The original Chinese texts in this present collection are based on the version of Zhu Xi's *Sishu zhangju jizhu* (Beijing: Zhonghua shuju, 2011). The commentator provides the textual interpretations in plain words, besides a title added to each entry. It is our hope that, through our efforts, the essential thoughts in *Daxue* and *Zhongyong* can be comprehensively accessible, and the core values in these two books can be more inspirational for readers of our generation and in the future.

目　录

大学选译

Contents

Higher Education (Selections)

中庸选译

The Universal Order (Selections)

大學選譯

Higher Education (Selections)

大学“三纲领”

“Three Guidelines” of Higher Education

1. 大学“三纲领”

【原文】

大学之道，在明明德，在亲民，在止于至善。

《大学·经》

【释文】

大学的宗旨在于使学者彰显光明的德性，在于使学者弃旧图新，在于使学者努力追求并最终达到最完善的道德境界。

【解析】

大学的宗旨这三句话，被称作大学的“三纲领”，其实质是为了使学者完善人格，“精神成人”。与功利性的“专业成才”相比，培养健全人格的“精神成人”更为重要。

1. "Three Guidelines" of Higher Education

【Text】

The object of a Higher Education is to bring out the intelligent moral power of our nature; to make a new and better society; and to enable us to abide in the highest excellence.

Higher Education · The Text of Confucius

【Commentary】

These opening lines, known as the "Three Guidelines" of Higher Education, are essential for the intellectuals to cultivate and perfect their character, because "reaching spiritual adulthood" is even more important than the utilitarian pursuit of "becoming a professional in career."

2. 知止而后有定

【原文】

知止而后有定，定而后能静，静而后能安，安而后能虑，虑而后能得。

《大学·经》

【释文】

知道应达到的道德境界然后才能有坚定的志向，志向坚定然后才能镇静不躁，镇静不躁然后才能内心安宁，内心安宁然后才能思虑周详，思虑周详然后才能有所收获。

【解析】

在大学求学，首先当“知其所止”，即明确自己应当努力追求并最终达到怎样的道德境界。有了明确的目标，才会有坚定的志向，坚强的决心，坚毅的意志，坚固的定力，学习才会有收获，有成就。

2. A standard of excellence brings out a fixed and definite purpose

【Text】

When a man has a standard of excellence before him, and only then, will he have a fixed and definite purpose; with a fixed and definite purpose, and only then, will he be able to have peace and tranquility of mind; with tranquility of mind, and only then, will he be able to have peace and tranquility of soul; with peace and serenity of soul, and only then, can he devote himself to deep, serious thinking and reflection; and it is only by deep, serious thinking and reflection that a man can attain true culture.

Higher Education · The Text of Confucius

【Commentary】

Those who seek knowledge in Higher Education should, first and foremost, possess "a standard of excellence." He should understand that to reach the highest moral excellence requires unswerving efforts. Ambition, resolution, tenacity and consistency will come along with a fixed purpose. Only then, will he reap what he sows in his study.

物有本末，事有终始

Causes and effects in physical nature;
springs of actions and consequences in human affairs

3. 物有本末，事有终始

【原文】

物有本末，事有终始。知所先后，则近道矣。

《大学·经》

【释文】

每种事物都有本有末，每件事情都有始有终。明白了这本末终始（孰重孰轻，孰先孰后）的道理（知道做事情的轻重缓急），就大体把握住大学的宗旨了。

【解析】

做事要分清轻重缓急。在大学学习，最根本的任务就是“精神成人”。学者应以“精神成人”引领“专业成才”。

3. Causes and effects in physical nature; springs of actions and consequences in human affairs

【Text】

In physical nature, there are causes and effects. In human affairs, there are springs of actions and consequences. When a man knows that he must first attend to the one before he can deal with the other, he is then not far from the truth.

Higher Education · The Text of Confucius

【Commentary】

The order of priority matters a great deal. For those seeking knowledge in Higher Education, the fundamental task is to "reach spiritual adulthood," by which the intellectuals should, then, grow to be "professionals in their careers."

4. 大学“八条目”

【原文】

格物—致知—诚意—正心—修身—齐家—治国—平天下。

《大学·经》

【释文】

接触和研究万事万物——从学习和研究中广泛地获取知识——使自己的意念真诚——使自己的心思端正——修养好自己的品性——整治好自己的家庭——治理好国家——治理天下使天下太平。

【解析】

这八句话是实现“三纲领”的“八条目”，是后人根据《大学》原文概括出来的。“八条目”的顺序是这样的：通过对万事万物的接触和研究之后才能获得知识；获得知识之后意念才能真诚；意念

4. "Eight Particulars" of Higher Education

【Text】

A systematic study of things — Acquire knowledge and understanding — Get true ideas — Put the minds in a proper and well-ordered condition — Order the conversation aright — Put the house in order — Secure good government in the country — Further the cause of enlightenment and civilization in the world.

Higher Education · The Text of Confucius

【Commentary】

In order to fulfill the "Three Guidelines," later readers have extracted the "Eight Particulars" from the original texts, which should be carried out in this manner: After a systematic study of things, and only then, knowledge and understanding will come. When knowledge and understanding have come, and only then, will men have true ideas. When men have true ideas, and only then, will their minds be in a proper and well-ordered condition. When men's minds are in a proper and well-ordered condition, and only then, will their conversation be ordered aright. When men's conversations are ordered aright, and only then, will their houses be kept in order. When men's houses are kept in order, and

真诚之后心思才能端正；心思端正之后才能修养好自己的品性；自己的品性修养好之后才能整治好自己的家庭；整治好自己的家庭之后才能治理好国家；治理好国家之后才能去治理天下使天下太平。三纲领，八条目，构成了一个完整的的思想体系，千百年来，一直是许多人，许多知识分子，甚至许多平民百姓的执着追求，是他们的人生观、价值观的重要内容，是他们崇高的精神信仰。在“三纲领”、“八条目”熏陶之下，许多读书人都具有强烈的历史使命感和高度的社会责任感，认为“天下兴亡，匹夫有责”（天下国家的兴亡，每个人都有责任），将“以天下为己任”（使天下国家太平是自己的责任和使命）作为自己的人生信条。

only then, will there be good government in the country. When there is good government in all countries, and only then, will there be peace and order in the world. Over thousands of years, this complete ideological system, consisting of the "Three Guidelines" and the "Eight Particulars," becomes a single-minded pursuit and sublime spiritual belief for many people, intellectuals and commoners alike. It dominates their outlook on life and value systems. As a result, a great many intellectuals have possessed a strong sense of historical mission and a high degree of social responsibility. And they believe in their lives that "all men share a common duty for the rise and fall of a nation" and "it is the duty and mission of every man to further the cause of peace and development of a nation."

修身为本

Order the conversation aright — the foundation

5. 修身为本

【原文】

自天子以至于庶人，壹是皆以修身为本。

《大学·经》

【释文】

上自天子，下至平民百姓，人人都要以修养自身品性为根本。

【解析】

在“八条目”中，“修身”为本，“修身”是最主要的条目，就好像一棵树，“修身”是它的根。“格物”，“致知”，“诚意”，“正心”，都是为了“修身”，是“培本”的功夫，好像水分和肥料，都是为了使根正苗壮。而“修身”，则是为今后成人成才茁壮成长奠定基础。因为只有在“修身”这个根基之上，才能进一步“齐家”(好像在根基上长成了粗壮的树干)，才能进一步“治国”，“平天下”(好像大树长满了枝叶，绽开了鲜花)，从而实现自己的理想与抱负。在大学求学，“修身”是根本，切不可本末倒置，更不可舍本逐末。

5. Order the conversation aright — the foundation

【Text】

From the Emperor down to the lowest of the common people, the one thing that all must do is to make the ordering of their conversation aright, the foundation for everything.

Higher Education · The Text of Confucius

【Commentary】

Among the "Eight Particulars," "ordering of the conversion aright" is the foundation for everything. And it can be likened to the root of a tree. "A systematic study of things," "acquire knowledge and understanding," "get true ideas," and "put the minds in a proper and well-ordered condition" are like water and fertilizer, without which the tree cannot take deep roots. Only when "ordering the conversation aright" is completed could "putting the house in order" (the tree trunk), "securing good government in the country" (branches), and "furthering the cause of enlightenment and civilization in the world" (flowers) be realized. Hence, one must not confuse the cause and the effect, for the "ordering of the conversation aright" is fundamental in fulfilling one's ideal and ambition.

6. 明明德

【原文】

《康诰》曰："克明德。"《大甲》曰："顾諟天之明命。"《帝典》曰："克明峻德。"皆自明也。

《大学·传首章》

【释文】

《尚书·周书·康诰》说："能够彰显光明的德性。"《尚书·商书·太甲》说："要重视这上天赋予的光明禀性。"《尚书·虞夏书·尧典》说："能够彰显崇高的德性。"这些都是说要自己彰显光明而崇高的德性。

【解析】

"三纲领"的第一条就是"明明德"（彰显光明的德性）。周初执政者很重视"德"。王国维说："中国政治与文化变革，莫剧于殷周之际。"（《殷周制度论》）殷与周，在政治思想观念上有很大不同，简言之，殷商"尊天事鬼"，而周则"敬德保民"。周初

6. Bring out the intelligent moral power of our nature

【Text】

The Commission of Investiture to Prince Kang says: "He (the Emperor Wen) succeeded in making manifest the power of his moral nature." In the *Address of the Minister I-Yin to the Emperor Tai Jia*, it is said: "He (the great Emperor Tang) kept constantly before him the clear Ordinance of God." In the *Memorial Record of the Emperor Yao*, it is said: "He succeeded in making manifest the lofty sublimity of his moral nature." Thus all these men made manifest the intelligent moral power of their nature.

Higher Education · Commentary I

【Commentary】

The first "Guideline" is "to bring out the intelligent moral power of our nature." Wang Guowei (1877—1927), a famous Chinese scholar, commented, "As for the political and cultural transformation in China, nothing is more drastic than that occurred during the transitional period between Yin and Zhou Dynasties." ("On the *Institutions of Yin and Zhou Dynasties*") These two dynasties vary a great deal in political thoughts: the former "respects the heaven and worships the ghosts," whereas the latter "values the moral nature and nurtures the people." During the early

的执政者认为，周王朝是靠“德”取得天下，也应靠“德”保有天下。“皆自明也”强调的是个体的主观精神，指明了要获得光明美好的道德，主要得依靠自己的努力。

period of Zhou Dynasty, its rulers put a high value on “moral nature.” They deemed that it was the “moral nature” that helped them attain and thereupon sustain sovereignty. The last sentence highlights the fact that to acquire the intelligent moral power of nature depends mainly on spiritual strength and individual efforts.

日新又新

Be new from day to day and everyday

7. 日新又新

【原文】

苟日新，日日新，又日新。

《大学·传二章》

【释文】

如果能够一天更新，就应天天更新，更新了还要再更新。

【解析】

这是汤之《盘铭》上的三句话。汤是殷商王朝开国之君，这三句话说明当一个王朝刚建立的时候，执政者总是力图除旧更新的。今天在大学求学的人，也应以此为座右铭，努力地不断地革故鼎新，弃旧图新，革除旧我，获得新生。

7. Be new from day to day and everyday

【Text】

Be a new man each day; from day to day, be a new man; every day, be a new man.

Higher Education · Commentary II

【Commentary】

This line is taken from *The Inscription on the Emperor Tang's Bath*. Tang was the first Emperor of Yin Shang Dynasty. While establishing a new regime, the rulers strive for exchanging the old for the new. Those who seek knowledge in Higher Education should take this line as a motto. Only by forsaking the past and starting afresh could the self-regeneration be accomplished.

8. 其命维新

【原文】

周虽旧邦，其命维新。

《大学·传二章》

【释文】

周王朝虽然是旧的邦国，但却禀受了新的天命。

【解析】

“三纲领”的第二条就是“亲民”（使人弃旧图新）。武王革命，推翻了商纣王，建立了周王朝。新王朝力图除旧更新：个人有新的道德，社会有新的风气，政治有新的举措，国家有新的面貌，整个社会欣欣向荣。

8. A new mission was given

【Text】

Royal House of Chou was an old State, a new Mission was given to it.

Higher Education · Commentary II

【Commentary】

The second "Guideline" is "to make a new and better society" (forsake the past and start afresh). The revolution started by Emperor Wu overthrew the ruling of Emperor Zhou of the Shang Dynasty, and helped the former establish the Zhou Dynasty. This guideline applies naturally to a new dynasty: for the individuals, there will be new moral standards; the society, new ethos; the politics, new measures; the nation, new looks; and a scene of prosperity will spread out through the whole society.

9. 知其所止

【原文】

于止，知其所止，可以人而不如鸟乎！

《大学·传三章》

【释文】

谈到居止，人就应当知道自己的归宿。连黄鸟都知道它该栖息在什么地方，难道人还可以不如一只鸟儿吗！

【解析】

“止”意为“居止”，是人们要到达并留居的地方。正如民有住房、鸟有归巢一样，作为毕生安身立命之所，每一个人也应当有精神上的追求，寻求最终的精神归宿。这种精神追求，其实就是信仰。“三纲领”的第三条明确提出，学者应“止于至善”，就是要将“至善”作为精神信仰并终身追求。

9. Know what to choose for the abode

【Text】

In choosing their abode, even the birds know what to choose. Can it be that man is less intelligent than birds!

Higher Education · Commentary III

【Commentary】

A bird flies back to its nest and a person returns home. Likewise, each and every scholar should seek an ultimate spiritual home, where his soul could be entrusted. This spiritual pursuit matches the third "Guideline" that a scholar must "abide in the highest excellence," and it should be the faith that scholars maintain in their lifelong efforts.

止于至善

Abide in the highest excellence

10. 止于至善

【原文】

为人君，止于仁；为人臣，止于敬；为人子，止于孝；为人父，止于慈；与国人交，止于信。

《大学·传三章》

【释文】

作为国君，要做到仁爱；作为臣子，要做到恭敬；作为子女，要做到孝顺；作为父亲，要做到慈爱；与国人交往，要做到诚信。

【解析】

"至善"就是"最好"，"极好"，指道德最崇高的境界。这里揭示了"至善"的具体内容，包括"仁""敬""孝""慈""信"。此外还包括执政者的政治伦理与道德操守："贤贤""亲亲"与"乐民""利民"，等等。汉代以"仁""义""礼""智""信"为"五常"。今天，"五常"对于我们，也同布帛菽粟一样，是不可须臾离开的东西：仁——仁者爱人，仁的意思爱人，是要爱父母长辈，

10. Abide in the highest excellence

【Text】

As a ruler, his ideal was to love mankind. As a subject, his ideal was to respect authority. As a son his ideal was to be a dutiful son. As a father, his ideal was to be kind to his children. In intercourse with his fellow men, his ideal was to be faithful and true.

Higher Education · Commentary III

【Commentary】

The "highest excellence" means the "best" and "extreme goodness." It refers to the highest level of moral state. Specifically, this entry shows us that "humanity," "respects," "filial piety," "kindness" and "trust" are all included in this "highest excellence." Equally important are the political ethics and moral integrity of men in authority, such as "promoting the talents," "respecting the relatives," "bring happiness and benefits to people," etc. In Han Dynasty, "humanity," "honor and duty," "rituals," "intelligence" and "trust" were regarded as the "Five Moral Qualities." To date, they are as important as daily necessities, without which we could not live even for one moment. "Humanity": A moral man loves all human beings. He loves his parents and seniors, his brothers and sisters, his friends and other strangers. He loves the general

爱兄弟姐妹，进而爱朋友，爱他人，爱民众，爱国家，爱大自然，爱我们人类赖以生存的家园。义——义者，宜也，义的意思是适宜、恰当，做事要恰当合理，讲道义，求真理，走正道，坚守公平正义。礼——礼即礼法制度，以及与之相适应的礼仪、礼俗、礼貌，在日常生活中，要讲文明，有礼貌，以礼待人，遵纪守法。智——智是智慧，重在明辨是非，分清善恶，从而决定取舍。信——信是诚实守信，表里如一，言行一致，重然诺，讲信用，言必信，行必果，有诚意，无二心，待人忠诚，不搞欺蒙诈骗。两千年来，仁义礼智信这“五常”成了中国人主要的精神追求与道德规范，是中国人不可摧毁的精神信仰。仁义礼智信实为中华民族优秀文化传统的核心和精髓。

public, the nation, the nature and the earth on which we are dwelling. "Honor and duty" denote a sense of appropriateness, and imply that one needs to take the apposite and appropriate measures in doing everything, especially in the pursuit of truth. One also must maintain the principles of fairness and justice. "Ritual" means the ceremonial rituals, proprieties, and usages of social life. One should be civil, treat others politely and obey the rules and regulations. "Intelligence": It is important to be able to tell right from wrong, and be clear about what is good and what is evil, so as to make the correct decision. "Trust" means being honest and truthful. What one says and does should correspond with what is on one's mind. One must be true in word and resolute in deed. One also should treat people sincerely and never deceive others. Over two thousand years, these "Five Moral Qualities" have become the predominant spiritual ideals, moral norms as well as the unswerving faith for Chinese people. They represent the core values of Chinese culture and traditions.

如切如磋，如琢如磨

“Cut and filed”, “chiseled and ground”

11. 如切如磋，如琢如磨

【原文】

如切如磋者，道学也；如琢如磨者，自修也；瑟兮僩兮者，恂栗也；赫兮喧兮者，威仪也；有斐君子，终不可諠兮者，道盛德至善，民之不能忘也。

《大学·传三章》

【释文】

这里所说的“如切如磋”，是说他如何求学治学；这里所说的“如琢如磨”，是说他如何自我修炼；这里所说的“瑟兮僩兮”，是说他对人谦恭，处事谨慎而有所戒惧；这里所说的“赫兮喧兮”，是说他仪表威严而举止文雅；这里所说的“有斐君子，终不可諠兮”，是说他由于品德非常高尚，达到了最完善的境界，所以民众不能忘怀。

【解析】

一个有志于“治国平天下”的君子，应努力完善自己的道德和才能，努力服务社会，造福人民，这样才能获得民众拥戴。

11. "Cut and filed", "chiseled and ground"

【Text】

The words "cut and filed" refer to the care that he took to improve his knowledge. The words "chiseled and ground" refer to the care that he took to make himself perfect. The words "how distinguished and calm he looks" show the seriousness of his mind. The words "how majestic and grand his air" show the dignity of his manners. Lastly, the words, "So full of grace is he — our Prince, Oh! His glory will never end," means that when glorious moral qualities are brought to such perfection, the people will never forget them.

Higher Education · Commentary III

【Commentary】

A moral man who aims to establish a good government in his own country and further peace and order throughout the world should strive for development of his moral character, serve the society and care about the welfare of his people. Only by doing so could he win the support and respect from his subjects.

12. 必也使无讼乎

【原文】

听讼，吾犹人也，必也使无讼乎！

《大学·传四章》

【释文】

审理案件，我也同别人一样，没有什么不同，要说不同，我只希望一定要让大家没有诉讼，人人和睦相处才好。

【解析】

这是孔子说的一句话。在孔子看来，在审理案子时，审明案情，分清是非，明确责任，准确量刑，当然十分重要，但更重要的是：一、社会上人人如能提高道德水准，就会减少案子的发生，甚至达到“无讼”的境地；二、执政者或执法者如能提高自身的道德水准，以自身正大光明的品德使人心产生敬畏，也会减少案子的发生，或使案件的审理得以顺利进行。这句话也可用来说明“修身”的重要。人们常说，治标不如治本。抓住了“修身”，就是抓住了根本，这样一来，一切也就会顺理成章了。

12. Try to make lawsuits impossible

【Text】

In deciding lawsuits, I am not better than other men. But what I make it a point to do is — I try to make lawsuits impossible.

Higher Education · Commentary IV

【Commentary】

This line is a quote from Confucius. It is significant, according to Confucius, that a judge must conduct the trial impartially, and impose punishment in a fair and just manner, but what is more important is this: 1. If more and more people with high moral standards could appear in the society, there would be fewer lawsuits, and even the goal of "making lawsuits impossible" would not be unable to be achieved. 2. If the politicians and judges could raise their moral standards, the number of the lawsuits would decrease or at least the trials could have been conducted smoothly. This quote indicates the importance of "self-cultivation." As to the lawsuits issues, to attach importance to the "self-cultivation" is to address both the symptoms and the root cause.

致知在格物

To acquire knowledge depends on a systematic study of things

13. 致知在格物

【原文】

所谓致知在格物者，言欲致吾之知，在即物而穷其理也。

《大学·传五章》

【释文】

所谓获得知识的途径在于接触和探究万事万物，是说要想获得知识，就在于接触万事万物而深入钻研彻底探究它的道理。

【解析】

“格物致知”的意思是，要接触和探究世界上的万事万物，才能获取知识，换句话说，要获取知识，必须接触和探究世界上的万事万物。“格”和“即”都有“接近”“接触”的意思，“即物”就是“格物”。今天在大学求学，学习书本知识，应当联系实际，并且重视亲身实践。

13. To acquire knowledge depends on a systematic study of things

【Text】

What is meant by "to acquire knowledge and understanding depends on a systematic study of things" is this: Knowledge and understanding could only be acquired when we get to know all matters and investigate the principles of them.

Higher Education · Commentary V

【Commentary】

This entry tells us that we must get to know and study systematically all matters in the world so as to acquire new knowledge. "Getting to know all matters" implies "a systematic study of all matters." We should study the world not only from books but also from real practice of our own.

14. 理有未穷而知有不尽

【原文】

人心之灵莫不有知，而天下之物莫不有理，惟于理有未穷，故其知有不尽也。是以“大学”始教，必使学者即凡天下之物，莫不因其已知之理而益穷之，以求至乎其极。

《大学·传五章》

【释文】

人心灵巧无不具有认知能力，而天下万事万物无不具有一定的道理，只不过因为这些道理还没有被人彻底探究，所以人们的知识就显得很有局限。因此，“大学”一开始就教求学者接触和探究天下万事万物，他们没有人不是凭借自己已有的知识去进一步探究，以求彻底认识万事万物的道理。

【解析】

在大学求学，既要好好读书，获取知识，又要联系实际或亲身实践，接触和探究世界上的万事万物，两者是统一的，不可把两者绝对地对立起来。

14. So long as all principles are not investigated, man's knowledge is incomplete

【Text】

The intelligent mind of mankind is certainly formed to know and there is not a single thing in which its principles are not inherent. But so long as all principles are not investigated, man's knowledge is incomplete. On this account, the Higher Education, at the outset of its lessons, instructs the learner, in regard to all matters in the world, to proceed from what knowledge he has of their principles, and pursue his investigation of them, till he reaches the extreme.

Higher Education · Commentary V

【Commentary】

To acquire knowledge in Higher Education, one needs to draw indirect experience from reading books and to get direct experience by investigating all matters in real practice. It is important to balance study and practice, both of which are integral parts of a unity.

诚其意者，毋自欺

To have true ideas is to have no self-deception

15. 诚其意者，毋自欺

【原文】

所谓诚其意者，毋自欺也。如恶恶臭，如好好色，此之谓自谦。故君子必慎其独也。

《大学·传六章》

【释文】

所谓使意念真诚、诚实，意思是说不要自己欺骗自己。就好像厌恶腐臭难闻的气味，又好像喜爱容貌美丽的女子，一切都自然地发自内心。这就叫作出自内心真诚而心安理得。所以，品德高尚的君子哪怕是在一个人独处的时候，也一定举止谨慎，言行不苟。

【解析】

诚意是要使意念真诚，做人诚实，不自欺欺人。从本质上来说，“诚意”是信仰问题。如果真心信仰，就不会口是心非，言行不一，明里一套，暗里一套，而是一心一意去追求，表现出信仰的虔诚。“慎独”是说一个人独处时也要敬慎，不要改变自己恒定的道德操守。在无人注视或监督的独处之时，一个人的所作所为，最容易看出他的精神信仰是否虔诚，道德品质是否高尚。

15. To have true ideas is to have no self-deception

【Text】

Now what is meant by "to have true ideas" is to have no self-deception, as when one hates a bad smell or loves what is beautiful. That is what is called self-detachment. Therefore a gentleman watches diligently over his secret thought.

Higher Education · Commentary VI

【Commentary】

"To have true ideas" means that one needs to be sincere in thoughts. Being honest, one does not deceive oneself as well as others. With true ideas, there will be no such thing as mouth specious and mind perverse, or the contradiction between words and acts. Instead, one will wholeheartedly pursue the true ideas, if one takes "to have true ideas" seriously and piously the way a religious devotee treats his faith. The last sentence implies that one, while being alone, must be prudent and consistently maintain the moral integrity. From what a man does when others are not present and watching, we can easily tell whether he is loyal to his spiritual faith and whether he has a noble moral character.

16. 富润屋，德润身

【原文】

富润屋，德润身，心广体胖。故君子必诚其意。

《大学·传六章》

【释文】

财富可以装饰房屋，品德却可以修养身心，使心胸宽广而体态舒泰安详。所以，品德高尚的君子一定要使自己的意念真诚、诚实。

【解析】

人们往往重视“富润屋”，轻忽“德润身”。但恰是后一句“德润身”，才更能彰显一个人的高贵与美丽。

16. Wealth embellishes a house, moral qualities embellish the person

【Text】

Wealth embellishes a house, but moral qualities embellish the person. When the mind is free and easy, the body will grow in flesh. Therefore a gentleman must have true ideas.

Higher Education · Commentary VI

【Commentary】

We are used to overemphasizing the fact that "wealth embellishes a house," but ignoring the truth that "moral qualities embellish the person." Yet a person's moral qualities can best demonstrate his or her nobility and beauty.

修身在正其心

Ordering conversation aright depends upon
putting the state of mind in a proper and well-ordered condition

17. 修身在正其心

【原文】

所谓修身在正其心者，身有所忿懥，则不得其正；有所恐惧，则不得其正；有所好乐，则不得其正；有所忧患，则不得其正。

《大学·传七章》

【释文】

所谓修养自身的品性要先端正自己的心思，是因为有所愤怒，心就不能够端正；有所恐惧，心就不能够端正；有所喜好，心就不能够端正；有所忧虑，心就不能够端正。

【解析】

为什么"修身"必先正其心？"心"，这里指的是人的意念，人的情绪，人的专注力。人是有情感的动物，人的愤怒、恐惧、喜乐、忧患之情，都会影响人的专注力，使人"分心"；极端的情绪，往往使人不能专注于"修身"。"心不在焉，视而不见，听而不闻……"，以至偏离"止于至善"的目标。因此，"正心"实为"修身"之前提。

17. Ordering conversation aright depends upon putting the state of mind in a proper and well-ordered condition

【Text】

Now what is meant by saying that the ordering of one's conversation aright depends upon putting the state of the mind in a proper and well-ordered condition, is this. When a person is under the influence of passion, his mind is not in a proper and well-ordered condition. When he is under the influence of fear and terror, his mind is not in a proper and well-ordered condition. When he is under the influence of pleasure and amusement, his mind is not in a proper and well-ordered condition. When he is under the influence of sorrow and distress, his mind is not in a proper and well-ordered condition.

Higher Education · Commentary VII

【Commentary】

Why "putting the state of the mind in a proper and well-ordered condition" is a prerequisite? The "state of the mind" denotes here the thoughts, emotions and concentration of a person. Human beings are emotional, thus anger, fear, happiness and anxieties will all affect the mental focus and cause the distraction. Because "when the mind is absent, we look, but do not see; we hear but do not understand..."

如能经常保持中和的精神状态，不受外物干扰，不因一时的感情冲动而丧失理智，专心致志，心无旁骛，才能使“修身”日益趋进。

Therefore, we may not be able to focus on "self-cultivation" and "abide in the highest excellence." If a man could maintain the central balance in his moral nature, and avoid being disturbed by things outside himself, he will be very devoted and focused, thereby making gradual progress in his "self-cultivation."

18. 齐其家在修其身

【原文】

所谓齐其家在修其身者，人之其所亲爱而辟焉，之其所贱恶而辟焉，之其所畏敬而辟焉，之其所哀矜而辟焉，之其所敖惰而辟焉。故好而知其恶，恶而知其美者，天下鲜矣！

《大学·传八章》

【释文】

所谓整治好自己的家庭要先修养好自身，是因为人们对于自己所亲爱的人会过分偏爱，对于自己所厌恶的人会过分鄙视，对于自己所敬畏的人会过分推崇，对于自己所同情的人会过分怜悯，对于自己所轻视的人会过分简慢。因此，喜爱一个人却知道那人的缺点，讨厌一个人却又知道那人的优点，能这样全面看人的人天下少有啊！

【解析】

整治家庭最重要的是持守中正，保持中和。对待家人和家事，不能任凭个人情感上的好恶而产生偏心，以至出现偏向、偏差与偏颇。

18. Putting one's house in order depends upon the ordering of his conversation aright

【Text】

Now what is meant by saying that putting one's house in order depends upon the ordering of his conversation aright, is this. Men are biased towards those for whom they feel love and affection; biased towards those whom they despise and dislike; biased towards those of whom they stand in awe and reverence; biased towards those for whom they feel pity and compassion; biased towards those towards whom they feel arrogance and pride. Wherefore it is that there are few men in the world who love and yet know the bad qualities of those whom they love; who hate and yet know the good qualities of those whom they hate.

Higher Education · Commentary VIII

【Commentary】

It is important to maintain the central point while putting one's house in order. To treat family members and deal with family issues, one must not depend on favoritism, lest bias occurs.

治国必先齐其家

Securing a good government depends firstly upon putting one's house in order

19. 治国必先齐其家

【原文】

所谓治国必先齐其家者，其家不可教而能教人者无之。故君子不出家而成教于国：孝者，所以事君也；弟者，所以事长也；慈者，所以使众也。

《大学·传九章》

【释文】

所谓治理国家必须先整治好自己的家庭，是因为不能管教好家人而能管教好国人的人，是没有的。所以，品德高尚的君子不出家门就能完成对国人的教育：因为他对父母的孝顺，可以用来侍奉君主；他对兄长的恭顺，可以用来侍奉官长；他对子女的慈爱，可以用来统率民众。

【解析】

"修身"是"齐家"的基础，而"齐家"又是"治国"的根基。

19. Securing a good government depends firstly upon putting one's house in order

【Text】

Now what is meant by saying that in order to have good government in the country, one must first put one's house in order, is this. He who cannot teach the members of his own family to be good can never teach other people to be good. Hence the moral man, without going out of his house, can learn the duties which he owes to the State. The duties of a good son will teach him how to serve his Sovereign. The duties of subordination in the family will teach him to respect authority. The kindness of a father to his children will teach him how to treat the multitude.

Higher Education · Commentary IX

【Commentary】

Self-cultivation, or ordering one's conversation aright, is the prerequisite for putting one's house in order, and securing a good government depends upon putting one's house in order. In ancient China, a family and a country shared remarkable similarities: a family is a small country, and a country is a large family. Men in authority can draw constructive experience from a successful practice of putting one's house in order. The family ethics can also be adapted and developed into

古代家国同构，家是小的国，国是大的家，齐家可为治国奠定基础，树立榜样，家庭伦理也可以拓展、演化为社会伦理、政治伦理。“孝”可与“忠”对接：在家能孝亲，在国就会忠君。“悌”可与“敬”对接：在家能敬兄，在外就会敬长。“慈幼”可与“爱民”对接：在家能慈爱幼小，在社会上就会爱护百姓。在这里，重要的是，在上位者要加强自身修养，处处起表率作用。

social and political ethics. "Filial piety" relates to "political loyalty": if one can be a good son at home, he will be a loyal servant for his master. "Brotherhood subordination" connects with "fraternal respects": a humble man who is respectful to his brothers at home will naturally respect the authority. "Parenting the children" associates with "loving the people": if one can be a caring parent at home, he will love and protect the people. Most importantly, man in authority should not miss any chance for self-perfection and should always remember to be an exemplar.

20. 如保赤子

【原文】

《康诰》曰："如保赤子。"心诚求之，虽不中，不远矣。

《大学·传九章》

【释文】

《尚书·周书·康诰》说："作为国君，保护平民百姓要像父母养护婴儿一样。"只要内心真诚地去追求，即使达不到目标，也不会相差太远。

【解析】

这里讲的是"慈幼"与"爱民"的对接：在上位的人在家如能慈爱幼小，在社会上就会"爱民如子"，爱护百姓。

20. As a mother watches over her new born child

【Text】

The *Commission of Investiture to Prince Kang* says: "Watch over the people as a mother watches over her new born child." A mother who seeks with her whole heart the good of her child, although she makes mistakes, will never go wholly wrong.

Higher Education · Commentary IX

【Commentary】

The text associates the performance of "parenting the children" with that of "loving the people." When those in authority could be good parents at home, they will watch over the people and love them the way they love their own children.

一家仁，一国兴仁

Kindness and humanity in one family,
the whole nation grows kind and humane

21. 一家仁，一国兴仁

【原文】

一家仁，一国兴仁；一家让，一国兴让；一人贪戾，一国作乱。其机如此。此谓一言偾事，一人定国。

《大学·传九章》

【释文】

如果一家是仁爱的，一国也会兴起仁爱之风；如果一家是礼让的，一国也会兴起礼让之风；如果有一人贪婪暴戾，一国就会发生动乱。其先兆就是这样清楚。这就叫作说错一句话就会使事情败坏，端正一个人就能使国家安定。

【解析】

“家风”会影响“国风”。在上位的人的所作所为往往对家庭和国家造成很大的甚至是决定性的影响。

21. Kindness and humanity in one family, the whole nation grows kind and humane

【Text】

When there is kindness and humanity in one family, the whole nation will grow kind and humane. When there is courtesy and politeness in one family, the whole nation will all become polite and courteous. The ambition and perversity of one man, on the other hand, may bring to confusion and anarchy the whole nation. Such is the power of influence. Hence the saying: "One word can ruin everything; one man can save a nation."

Higher Education · Commentary IX

【Commentary】

The "ethos of a family" will affect the "ethos of a nation." More often than not, what those in authority do and how they behave will exercise a strong, sometimes decisive, influence upon the family and the society.

22. 治国在齐其家

【原文】

君子有诸己而后求诸人，无诸己而后非诸人。所藏乎身不恕，而能喻诸人者，未之有也。故治国在齐其家。

《大学·传九章》

【释文】

品德高尚的君子，总是自己先具有了美德然后才要求别人具有美德，自己先除掉了自身的恶习然后才能批评别人的恶习。如果本身都不讲这种推己及人的恕道，而想教导别人也讲恕道，那是不可能办到的。所以，治理国家必须先整治好自己的家庭。

【解析】

在上位的人无论治家与治国，都应推己及人，以身作则。榜样的力量是无穷的。

22. To have a good government lies in putting one's house in order

【Text】

Before requiring any moral quality of the people, the ruler must himself have that moral quality; before condemning any vice in the people, he must himself be free of that vice. A man who does not consider his own moral condition can never influence others for good. Therefore government in a country depends upon putting one's house in order.

Higher Education · Commentary IX

【Commentary】

Whether manage a household or rule a nation, a man in authority must play an exemplary role. How powerful a good example is!

平天下在治其国

Have a good government and further the peace and order throughout the world

23. 平天下在治其国

【原文】

所谓平天下在治其国者，上老老而民兴孝；上长长而民兴弟；上恤孤而民不倍，是以君子有絜矩之道也。

《大学·传十章》

【释文】

所谓平治天下必须先治理好自己的国家，是因为在上位者尊敬老人，老百姓就会兴起孝敬父母之风；在上位者尊重长辈，老百姓就会兴起尊敬兄长之风；在上位者体恤救济孤儿，老百姓就不会背离而是跟着去做，所以品德高尚的君子有“絜矩之道”，总能推己及人以身作则。

【解析】

这里所说的“絜矩之道”，其实是“恕”道。所谓“恕”，是指宽容、厚道、仁慈、忍让，以仁爱之心待人，能推己及人，将心比心，处处为他人着想，并且处处以身示范，为人表率。己之所好，与人共之；己之所恶，切勿加之。这是一种爱心、同情心，是将家庭伦理（孝悌）放大到社会上而形成的社会伦理、政治伦理（忠恕）。

23. Have a good government and further the peace and order throughout the world

【Text】

Now what is meant by saying that peace and order throughout the world depend upon having good government in one's own country, is this. When those in authority honor old age, the people will become dutiful sons. When those in authority respect and obey their superiors, the people will all become good citizens. When those in authority take care of the poor and helpless, the people will not neglect them. Thus a gentleman has a self-measuring rule.

Higher Education · Commentary X

【Commentary】

The so called "self-measuring rule" here refers actually to the "charity rule." By "charity," it means tolerance, mercifulness, benevolence, and forbearance. Treat others as one expects to be treated, think into others' minds, and be strict with oneself so as to establish an exemplar for others. Practice what one preaches, and share what one loves. Whatsoever things you do not wish that others should do unto you, do not do unto them. It is a kind of love and sympathy. The family ethics (filial piety) has thus been developed into the social and political ethics (loyalty and charity).

24. 絜矩之道

【原文】

所恶于上，毋以使下；所恶于下，毋以事上；所恶于前，毋以先后；所恶于后，毋以从前；所恶于右，毋以交于左；所恶于左，毋以交于右。此之谓絜矩之道。

《大学·传十章》

【释文】

如果厌恶上司对你的态度，就不要用这种态度去对待你的下属；如果厌恶下属对你的态度，就不要用这种态度去对待你的上司；如果厌恶在你前面的人对你的态度，就不要用这种态度对待在你后面的人；如果厌恶在你后面的人对你的态度，就不要用这种态度去对待在你前面的人；如果厌恶在你右边的人对你的态度，就不要用这种态度去对待在你左边的人；如果厌恶在你左边的人对你的态度，就不要用这种态度去对待在你右边的人。这就叫作推己及人、以身作则、在道德上示范于人的“絜矩之道”。

【解析】

践行“絜矩之道”（即“恕”道），重在推己及人，将心比心，处处为他人着想，并且处处以身示范，为人表率。

24. A self-measuring rule

【Text】

What a man hates in the conduct of those who are above him, let him not show it in his treatment of those who are under him. What he hates in the conduct of those who are under him, let him not show it when doing his duty to those who are above him. What he hates in the conduct of those who go before him, let him not be the first to show in dealing with those who come after him. What he hates in the conduct of those who come after him, let him not follow their example and show in dealing with those who go before him. What he hates in the conduct of those who are on the right hand of him, let him not show in dealing with those who are on the left hand of him. What he hates in the conduct of those who are on the left hand of him, let him not show in dealing with those who are on the right hand of him. This is what is called a self-measuring rule.

Higher Education · Commentary X

【Commentary】

To abide by the "self-measuring rule," it is critical to treat others as one expects to be treated, to think into others' minds, and to be strict with oneself so as to establish an exemplar for others.

25. 乐只君子，民之父母

【原文】

《诗》云：“乐只君子，民之父母。”民之所好好之，民之所恶恶之。此之谓民之父母。

《大学·传十章》

【释文】

《诗经·小雅·南山有台》说：“多么快乐的国君啊，你是老百姓的父母。”老百姓喜爱的，他也喜爱；老百姓厌恶的，他也厌恶。这样的国君就可以说是老百姓的父母了。

【解析】

这就是“与民同欲”的意思。古人认为，处在上位的执政者对待处在下位的民众，应该像父母疼爱自己的子女那样，关心他们，养育他们，疼爱他们，保护他们。

25. How the people love the prince who is a father and a mother to the people

【Text】

The *Book of Songs* says: "How the people love the prince who is a father and a mother to the people!" To love what the people love and to hate what the people hate: that is what is meant by being a father and a mother to the people.

Higher Education · Commentary X

【Commentary】

"Love and hate what the people love and hate." A ruler should treat his people in the way that parents love, care, nurture and protect their own children.

得众则得国，失众则失国

When a ruler gains the hearts of the people, he will gain the kingdom;
when he loses the hearts of the people, he will lose the kingdom

26. 得众则得国，失众则失国

【原文】

道得众则得国，失众则失国。

《大学·传十章》

【释文】

国君有道，得到民心就能得到国家，国君无道，失去民心就会失去国家。

【解析】

战国时期思想家荀子曾说，国君像船，人民像水，水可以把船浮起来，也可以把船掀翻。

26. When a ruler gains the hearts of the people, he will gain the kingdom; when he loses the hearts of the people, he will lose the kingdom

【Text】

When a ruler gains the hearts of the people, he will gain the kingdom; when he loses the hearts of the people, he will lose the kingdom.

Higher Education · Commentary X

【Commentary】

An ancient Chinese philosopher Xunzi (313—238B.C.) once commented, a ruler can be likened to a boat, and people the water. A boat can float on the water, yet the waves can also turn the boat upside down.

君子先慎乎德

The first care of the ruler is to make sure that he has the moral qualities

27. 君子先慎乎德

【原文】

是故君子先慎乎德。有德此有人，有人此有土，有土此有财，有财此有用。

《大学·传十章》

【释文】

品德高尚的君子首先要认真谨慎地修养品德。有良好的品德才会有人拥护，有人拥护才能保有土地，有土地才会有财富，有财富才能有钱物使用。

【解析】

孔子主张以德治国，实行德治。“德”有“道德”和“恩德”两种含义。孔子认为，实行“德治”，首要任务是在物质上给民众以恩惠（惠民）；其次，在精神上执政者要提高道德修养（爱民），并重视对民众的道德教育（化民）。这样做，天下就会大治。

27. The first care of the ruler is to make sure that he has the moral qualities

【Text】

Therefore the first care of the ruler is to make sure that he has the moral qualities. Who has the moral qualities, has the people; who has the people, has the land; who has the land, has the revenue; who has the revenue, has the power to use it.

Higher Education · Commentary X

【Commentary】

Confucius upheld the idea of ruling a nation with moral natures. The meanings of the Chinese character "*de*" (morality) can be twofold: 1. moral quality, or virtue; 2. favor, or grace. To put this idea into practice, Confucius thought, a ruler should, first and foremost, bring material benefits to the people; next, a ruler should improve his moral development; finally, he should also take into serious consideration the moral education for the people. Only by doing so could peace and prosperity be spread out across the whole world.

28. 德本财末

【原文】

德者，本也；财者，末也。

《大学·传十章》

【释文】

品德啊，这是根本；财富啊，这是枝末。

【解析】

在上位的人要分清本末，不可本末倒置。应将修养品德视为根本，放在首位，切不可见利忘义，疯狂敛财。

28. Moral quality, the foundation; wealth, the means

【Text】

Moral qualities are the foundation of a nation. Wealth is but the means.

Higher Education · Commentary X

【Commentary】

Those in authority must not put the cart before the horse. The cultivation of moral character, the foundation of a nation, should be prioritized. It is wrong to accumulate wealth in an unrestricted and unscrupulous manner.

29. 财散民聚

【原文】

财聚则民散，财散则民聚。

《大学·传十章》

【释文】

国君聚敛财富，民心就会离散；国君散财于民，民心就会凝聚。

【解析】

这是一条重要的历史经验，也是一个颠扑不破的真理。

29. The distribution of wealth among the many contributes to the stability of society

【Text】

The accumulation of wealth in a few hands leads to the dissolution of society, while the distribution of wealth among the many contributes to the stability of society.

Higher Education · Commentary X

【Commentary】

This is a significant experience from history as well as an irrefutable truth.

仁人能爱人能恶人

The truly good and moral man can love or hate others

30. 仁人能爱人能恶人

【原文】

唯仁人为能爱人，能恶人。

《大学·传十章》

【释文】

有仁德的君子爱憎分明，能明确地喜好善人，能明确地厌恶恶人。

【解析】

仁者不是是非善恶不分的好好先生。由于仁者以“仁”为标准来识别是非善恶，所以就会有正确的好恶爱憎。

30. The truly good and moral man can love or hate others

【Text】

It is only the truly good and moral man who can love or hate others.

Higher Education · Commentary X

【Commentary】

With a true moral standard, a moral man can tell right from wrong, and his perspectives on what he loves or hates are thus correct.

31. 忠信以得之，骄泰以失之

【原文】

是故君子有大道：必忠信以得之，骄泰以失之。生财有大道：生之者众，食之者寡，为之者疾，用之者舒，则财恒足矣。

《大学·传十章》

【释文】

因此，身为国君的君子治理国家有正确的途径：忠诚守信便一定会获得一切，骄恣放纵便一定会失去一切。增殖财富也有正确的途径：生产的人多，消费的人少；生产的人勤奋努力，消费的人节约用度。这样，财富便会经常充足。

【解析】

在上位的人治理国家，必须忠诚守信，兑现对百姓的承诺，如果骄奢淫逸，必自取灭亡。

31. If faithful and trustworthy, he is sure to succeed; if proud and careless, he is sure to fail

【Text】

Thus in life there is one great law for a gentleman. If faithful and trustworthy, he is sure to succeed; if proud and careless, he is sure to fail. In the same manner in the production of wealth there is one great law. When there are many who produce and few who consume; when those who work, work hard, and those who spend, spend slowly; then there will always be plenty of wealth in the nation.

Higher Education · Commentary X

【Commentary】

The man in authority, while ruling a country, should be faithful and trustworthy, and prove his commitment to the people. For a ruler, leading a voluptuous life is little more than a kiss of death.

32. 仁者以财发身，不仁者以身发财

【原文】

仁者以财发身，不仁者以身发财。未有上好仁而下不好义者也，未有好义其事不终者也，未有府库财非其财者也。

《大学·传十章》

【释文】

仁爱的人仗义疏财以成名起家，不仁的人不惜以生命为代价去敛钱发财。没有在上位的人喜好仁德而在下位的人却不喜好忠义的，没有喜好忠义而为国君做事却半途而废的，没有不将府库里的财物不是当成自己财物而加以保护的。

【解析】

孔子对“义”和“利”，有着非常辩证的看法。他认为居上位的“君子”，如果为谋一己之私利而抛弃道义，就会招致民众的怨恨。君子应该根据道义去“利民”，这样一来就会得到民众的拥护，这就叫作“以义为利”。长期以来，儒家都十分重视公私之分，义利之辨，认为这是修身和从政一个重要的原则问题。

32. Moral men make money to live; immoral men live to make money

【Text】

Moral men make money to live. Immoral men live to make money. You will never find where the rulers are human and kind that the people do not love honor and duty. You will never find where the people in a nation love honor and duty, that the affairs of that nation do not prosper, and that the wealth in the nation does not belong to the ruler.

Higher Education · Commentary X

【Commentary】

Confucius maintained a dialectic view towards the "moral qualities" and the "wealth." In particular, he advised the "moral men" in authority: bring benefits to the people and they will return their respect and support; whereas exploiting one's position for personal gains at the expense of honor and duty will only invite resentment from the people. And that is why the "honor and duty make a nation prosperous." The Confucian scholars have always kept in mind the dividing line between the public and the private, between the moral qualities and the material properties, for it is essential for self-cultivation and political governance.

以义为利

Honor and duty make a nation prosperous

33. 以义为利

【原文】

国不以利为利，以义为利也。

《大学·传十章》

【释文】

治理一个国家的君主不应该以财货为利益，而应该以仁义为利益。

【解析】

在上位的人不应聚敛财富，谋取私利，而应施行仁义，造福社会和人民。

33. Honor and duty make a nation prosperous

【Text】

What really makes a nation prosperous is not wealth and material prosperity, but honor and duty.

Higher Education · Commentary X

【Commentary】

Those in authority should not accumulate the wealth for personal gains, but bring benefits, in accordance with honor and duty, to the society and the people.

中庸選譯

The Universal Order (Selections)

天命之谓性

The ordinance of God is what we call the law of our being

1. 天命之谓性

【原文】

天命之谓性，率性之谓道，修道之谓教。

《中庸·第一章》

【释文】

人的自然禀赋（本然之善）叫作“性”，顺着本性去做（执中守正）叫作“道”，按照“道”的原则修身养性叫作“教”。

【解析】

这句意思是说，中庸（中和）之道原本就存在于天赋的本性中，为人性之所固有，顺着本性行事，就是正道、达道——中庸（中和）之道。人们据此修养自己和教化他人，就叫作“教”。人们应当重视本性中的本然之善（执中守正，折中致和），自觉地去保有它，养护它。

1. The ordinance of God is what we call the law of our being

【Text】

The ordinance of God is what we call the law of our being. To fulfill the law of our being is what we call the moral law. The moral law when reduced to a system is what we call religion.

The Universal Order · Chapter I

【Commentary】

The universal moral law (find the central balance in moral nature) is an inherent part of human nature. The right and universal way to fulfill the law of our being is to act according to our nature. To reduce the self-cultivation and teaching of others to a system is what we call religion. We should treasure and preserve this natural goodness (maintain the central point and guard the upright, keep the central balance and fulfill the moral sense).

2. 道不可须臾离

【原文】

道也者，不可须臾离也。

《中庸·第一章》

【释文】

“道”是不可以片刻离开的。

【解析】

中庸（中和）之道同我们每一个人都有非常密切的关系，像吃饭穿衣一样，在日常生活中我们不可以片刻离开它。

2. We cannot escape the operation of moral law for one instant in our existence

【Text】

The moral law is a law from whose operation we cannot for one instant in our existence escape.

The Universal Order · Chapter I

【Commentary】

The moral law is closely related to each and every one of us. It is as common as feeding and clothing oneself, and we cannot for one instant escape in our existence.

3. 中为天下之大本，和为天下之达道

【原文】

中也者，天下之大本也；和也者，天下之达道也。

《中庸·第一章》

【释文】

执中守正，是天下一切情感和道理的根本；折中致和，是天下一切事物的普遍原则。

【解析】

《中庸》从人的性情来阐释“中庸（中和）”之道。当“喜怒哀乐”未发之时，人的性情自然是中正不偏的，这就是“中”（是先天的禀赋）；而一旦接触了外物，有了“喜怒哀乐”之情，但抒发出来都合乎“执两用中”，并且“无过无不及”，这就是“和”，是后天教化所获。可见，“中庸（中和）”之道是天下一切情感和道理的根本，也是天下一切事物的普遍原则。

3. Moral being is the great reality existence; moral order is the universal law in the world

【Text】

Our true self or moral being is the great reality existence, and moral order is the universal law in the world.

The Universal Order · Chapter I

【Commentary】

The book *Zhongyong* explains "moral being" and "moral order" from the perspective of human emotions. When "happiness, anger, sadness or joy" is not generated, a man is true and impartial, and this is what "moral being (a natural endowment)" means; when those emotions are produced upon various occasions, a moral man can take the two extremes of negative and positive, and apply the mean of the two extremes. Moreover, he will either go beyond the mark, or not come up to it. And this is "moral order" which can be acquired by education and cultivation. Thus, the universal moral order is the basis of all emotions and principles. It is also the fundamental law for everything in the world.

致中和

To realize true moral being and moral order

4. 致中和

【原文】

致中和，天地位焉，万物育焉。

《中庸·第一章》

【释文】

达到“中和”的境界，天地便各在其位了，万物便生长繁育了。

【解析】

如果在宇宙万物中，在人类世界里，都能践行中庸（中和）之道，就会达到“天地位”和“万物育”的极致。这就是中庸（中和）之道的神功造化。

4. To realize true moral being and moral order

【Text】

When true moral being and moral order are realized, the universe then becomes a cosmos and all things attain their full growth and development.

The Universal Order · Chapter I

【Commentary】

In the world of human beings, if the universal moral order could be put into effect, "the universe then becomes a cosmos and all things attain their full growth and development." This is what the magic power of the universal moral order can bring.

君子中庸

The life of the moral man is an exemplification of the universal moral order

5. 君子中庸

【原文】

君子中庸，小人反中庸。

《中庸·第二章》

【释文】

君子总是按中庸行事，小人总是违背中庸。

【解析】

中庸（中和）之道可以作为分界线，来区分“君子”与“小人”。这是因为君子每时每刻都能持守中道，这是君子的操守。至于道德低下的“小人”，则是肆无忌惮地“反中庸”，他们情绪偏激，好走极端，露才扬己，肆意妄为。他们总是与中庸之道背道而驰。

5. The life of the moral man is an exemplification of the universal moral order

【Text】

The life of the moral man is an exemplification of the universal moral order. The life of the vulgar person, on the other hand, is a contradiction of the universal moral order.

The Universal Order · Chapter II

【Commentary】

According to the universal moral order, it is easy to draw a clear line of demarcation between a moral man and a vulgar person. A moral man of high integrity always maintains the universal order. Whereas a vulgar person unscrupulously goes against the moral order, and those who are paranoid, reckless and arrogant run counter to the universal moral order.

6. 君子而时中

【原文】

君子之中庸也，君子而时中。

《中庸·第二章》

【释文】

君子之所以总是按中庸行事，是因为君子总能因时制宜按照当时情况做到执中守正，无过无不及。

【解析】

道德高尚的“君子”，因为有君子之德，所以能“时中”，即“随时以处中”。也就是说，君子总能因时制宜，根据不同时间、不同地点、不同情况、不同条件，或执中守正，或折中致和，从而总能处在“不偏不倚”“无过无不及”的中正位置上。因此，君子每时每刻都能持守中道，这是君子的操守。

6. The moral man unceasingly cultivates his moral being

【Text】

The moral man's life is an exemplification of the universal order, because he is a moral person who unceasingly cultivates his true self or moral being.

The Universal Order · Chapter II

【Commentary】

A "moral man" with high moral standards unceasingly cultivates his true self or moral being. In other words, a moral man acts in line with time, places, conditions and scenarios; he maintains the central point and guards the upright, keeps the central balance and fulfills the moral sense; he situates himself in an impartial position, neither going beyond the mark nor not coming up to it. Hence, he can always maintain the universal moral order, for it is the integrity of a moral man.

7. 中庸其至矣乎

【原文】

中庸其至矣乎！

《中庸·第三章》

【释文】

中庸之道大概是最高的德行了吧！

【解析】

孔子认为中庸之德，是最高的境界，但一般人难于执守，往往不是“过”就是“不及”，“过则失中，不及则未至”（过则偏离了中，不及则未达到中），这是由于教化缺失所致，因此孔子发出深深的感叹。

7. To find and get into the true central balance of our moral being

【Text】

To find and get into the true central balance of our moral being, i.e. our true moral ordinary self, that indeed is the highest human attainment.

The Universal Order · Chapter III

【Commentary】

According to Confucius, the highest human attainment is to find and get into the true central balance of our moral being. However, most of us will either go beyond the mark, or do not come up to it. "To go beyond the mark leads to the deviation from the true central balance; whereas not to come up to the mark signifies a failure to attain the central balance." This results from a lack of education. No wonder Confucius sighed so sympathetically.

道之不行与不明

Why there is no real moral life and why the moral law is not understood

8. 道之不行与不明

【原文】

道之不行也，我知之矣，知者过之，愚者不及也。道之不明也，我知之矣，贤者过之，不肖者不及也。

《中庸·第四章》

【释文】

中庸之道不能实行的原因，我知道了，那些所谓“聪明过头”的人总是思想偏激看法过了头，而愚昧的人认识又跟不上因而不能理解它。中庸之道不能弘扬的原因，我知道了，那些所谓“贤能超群”的人总是做得太过分，而不贤的人根本做不到。

【解析】

孔子这番话，重在告诫人们，无论看问题还是做事情，须知“过犹不及”（“过头”和“赶不上”一样，都偏离了中道），因而不可偏激，不要走极端，而应从容适度，恪守中道。

8. Why there is no real moral life and why the moral law is not understood

【Text】

I know now why there is no real moral life. The wise mistake moral law for something higher than what it really is; and the foolish do not know enough what moral law really is. I know now why the moral law is not understood. The noble natures want to live too high, high above their moral ordinary self; and ignoble natures do not live high enough, i.e., not up to their moral ordinary true self.

The Universal Order · Chapter IV

【Commentary】

These words from Confucius are to warn people against going to extremes. One must scrupulously observe the moral order in one's thinking and action, taking the appropriate measure at a sedate pace (to go beyond the mark, or not to come up to it departs from the moral order).

舜好问而好察迩言，隐恶而扬善

Shun had a natural curiosity of mind and loved to inquire into near facts

9. 舜好问而好察迩言，隐恶而扬善

【原文】

舜好问而好察迩言，隐恶而扬善。

《中庸·第六章》

【释文】

舜喜欢向人问问题，又善于分析别人浅近话语里的含义。他待人宽厚，从不渲染别人的不善，但总是宣扬别人的善。

【解析】

“好问而好察迩言”，用今天的话来说就是善于调查研究，一切从实际出发。“隐恶而扬善”，则是宅心仁厚，有仁爱宽厚之心，厚德载物，能包容万物。

9. Shun had a natural curiosity of mind and loved to inquire into near facts

【Text】

Shun had a natural curiosity of mind and he loved to inquire into near facts. He looked upon evil merely as something negative; and he recognized only what was good as having a positive existence.

The Universal Order · Chapter VI

【Commentary】

The former part of this line suggests that we need to be skilled in inquiry and research, and proceeding from a realistic view in everything we do. The latter part emphasizes the importance of being moral, merciful, tolerant and generous.

10. 执其两端，用其中于民

【原文】

执其两端，用其中于民。

《中庸·第六章》

【释文】

舜善于掌握过与不及两端的意见及方方面面的情况，通过折中调和，确定中正恰当的决策，而施行于老百姓。

【解析】

“执其两端，用其中于民”，是说凡事都先弄清楚事物或问题两个极端（或对立的两个方面）的情况，弄清楚事物或问题方方面面的情况，然后通过折中调和，找出“中正”“中和”的办法，运用到民众身上，这就叫作“执两用中”，“折中致和”，无“过”也无“不及”，是中庸之道作为方法论的精髓。

10. Taking the two extremes of negative and positive, and applying the mean in the dealing with people

【Text】

Taking the two extremes of negative and positive, he (Shun) applied the mean between the two extremes in his judgment, employment and dealings with people.

The Universal Order · Chapter VI

【Commentary】

This line tells us to take into consideration of the opposite sides or two extremes of a problem, and also examine a problem from all angles. After that, we need to adopt the "mean measures" in accordance with the "moral order." This is what is called "maintaining the central point and guarding the upright," or "keeping the central balance and fulfilling the moral sense." There is either "going beyond the mark," or "not coming up to it." It is the essence of the universal moral order.

11. 择乎中庸，而不能期月守

【原文】

人皆曰“予知”，择乎中庸，而不能期月守也。

《中庸·第七章》

【释文】

人人都说“我很聪明，我都知道”，可是选择了中庸之道却连一个月的时间也不能坚持。

【解析】

中庸之道，重在践行。

11. Men are not able to keep the true central balance for a round month

【Text】

Men all say, "We are wise"; but in finding the true central clue and balance in their moral being and following the line of conduct which is in accordance with it, they are not able to keep it for a round month.

The Universal Order · Chapter VII

【Commentary】

It is important to find the true central balance in moral being and follow the line of conduct in accordance with the moral order.

拳拳服膺而弗失

Embrace it with all his might and never lost it again

12. 拳拳服膺而弗失

【原文】

回之为人也，择乎中庸，得一善，则拳拳服膺而弗失之矣。

《中庸·第八章》

【释文】

颜回的为人是这样的，他选择了中庸之道，只要得到了一点好处，就会把中庸之道牢记在心，诚恳信奉，再也不让它失去。

【解析】

颜回是孔子最优秀的学生，常受到孔子称赞。孔子说他选择了“中庸”，得“一善”，有了成效，便一辈子记住并终身奉行。颜回实为既能“明道”又能“行道”的典范。

12. Embrace it with all his might and never lost it again

【Text】

Hui was a man who all his life sought the central clue in his moral being, and when he got hold of one thing that was good he embraced it with all his might and never lost it again.

The Universal Order · Chapter VIII

【Commentary】

Yan Hui was one of the most excellent disciples of Confucius, and thus received frequent compliments from his master. Confucius pointed out that Yan sought "the central clue in his moral being" and got hold of "one good thing." And he embraced it with all his might and applied it through all his life. Yan Hui indeed set up a good example in "understanding and practicing" the universal moral order.

君子和而不流，中立而不倚

The moral man is independent without any bias

13. 君子和而不流，中立而不倚

【原文】

君子和而不流，强哉矫！中立而不倚，强哉矫！国有道，不变塞焉，强哉矫！国无道，至死不变，强哉矫！

《中庸·第十章》

【释文】

品德高尚的君子性情平和但不随波逐流，这才是真正的坚强啊！持守中正而不偏不倚，这才是真正的坚强啊！国家政治清平时不改变志向，这才是真正的坚强啊！国家政治黑暗时坚持操守，宁死不变，这才是真正的坚强啊！

【解析】

孔子弟子子路一向好勇逞强，孔子针对子路之问，提出“北方之强”与“南方之强”加以辨析，并告诉子路，应当“和而不流”，“中立而不倚”，任何时候都不改变原有的“中正”“中和”的操守，这才是真正的“强”。孔子曾说，君子有勇而无义就会搞叛乱，

13. The moral man is independent without any bias

【Text】

Wherefore the man with the true force of moral character is one who is easy and accommodating and yet without weakness or indiscrimination. How unflinchingly firm he is in his strength! He is independent without any bias. How unflinchingly firm he is in his strength! When there is moral social order in the country, if he enters public life he does not change from what he was when in retirement. When there is no moral social order in the country he holds on his way without changing even unto death. How unflinchingly firm he is in his strength!

The Universal Order · Chapter X

【Commentary】

Zilu, one of Confucius' disciples, was so fond of parading his valor and superiority. This entry is actually the answer provided by Confucius to a question from Zilu. Confucius thought, a moral man should be "easy and accommodating and yet without weakness or indiscrimination," and "independent without any bias." He must unswervingly maintain his integrity: "seeking the central point in moral being," or "abiding by

勇敢却不懂礼就会莽撞乱来。认为子路之“勇”，要用“礼义”来节制，回归中庸之道。

the universal moral order." This is what is called "unflinchingly firm strength." A gentleman who has valor, but is without the knowledge and love of what is right, is likely to commit a crime. Confucius thought, the valor from Zilu should not be overdeveloped, and only the "knowledge and love of what is right" can bring him back to the right track of moral order.

14. 遁世不见知而不悔

【原文】

君子依乎中庸，遁世不见知而不悔。

《中庸·第十一章》

【释文】

真正的君子总是遵循中庸之道坚持走下去，即使一生远离尘俗不被人知道也不后悔。

【解析】

君子依乎中庸，不去深求“隐僻”之理，不去故为“诡异”之行，遵道而行绝不半途而废，即使不为人知也终身不悔，显示了对中庸之道的执着追求。

14. Live unknown to the world and unnoticed of men without any concern

【Text】

There are truly moral men who unconsciously live a life in entire harmony with the universal moral order and who live unknown to the world and unnoticed of men without any concern.

The Universal Order · Chapter XI

【Commentary】

A moral man acts in line with the universal moral order. He seeks no principles that are "obscure and uncommon," and never attracts attention with "eccentric and heretic" deeds. He abides by the moral order and never gives up halfway. He will not regret it even if he lives unknown to the world and unnoticed of men. It shows that he persistently seeks the universal moral order.

君子之道费而隐

The moral law is to be found everywhere, and yet it is a secret

15. 君子之道费而隐

【原文】

君子之道，费而隐。君子之道，造端乎夫妇，及其至也，察乎天地。

《中庸·第十二章》

【释文】

君子所持守的中庸之道作用非常广泛而道理又非常精微。君子所持守的中庸之道，开始于普通男女的日常生活，但它的最高深境界却显耀于整个天地。

【解析】

君子之道，也就是中庸之道，运用极广，小到“夫妇居室”，大到“圣人天地”，无远弗届，无所不包。像鸟高飞蓝天，像鱼下潜深渊，持守中庸之道，可明察天地，洞悉万有。至于其义理，其浅近之处，“匹夫匹妇”皆能理解和运用；其深奥之处，即使是圣人也难完全破解领悟。从而告诉人们，不要因为其“道”浅近就轻忽它，也不要因为其“道”深奥就疏远它。

15. The moral law is to be found everywhere, and yet it is a secret

【Text】

The moral law is to be found everywhere, and yet it is a secret. The moral law takes its rise in the relation between man and woman; but in its utmost reaches, it reigns supreme over heaven and earth.

The Universal Order · Chapter XII

【Commentary】

The moral law is actually the moral order, which is universally applicable. Whether it is a space as small as a house in which a husband and a wife dwell, or a realm as vast as the world where men with perfect nature roam around, there is no place that the moral order could not reach, and there is nothing that the moral order does not include. With it, one is able to examine the heaven and the earth, and get to know all matters in the world. As for the meanings and implications, the moral order is so approachable that even the commoners can understand it and apply it to life; equally, the moral order is so profound that even the men with the most perfect divine nature could not completely get hold of it. Thus, we must not ignore "the moral order" because it is approachable, nor must we keep a distance from it because it is profound.

16. 道不远人

【原文】

道不远人。

《中庸·第十三章》

【释文】

中庸之道并不是远离人们的。

【解析】

中庸之道就在我们身边，我们一刻也不能离开它。

16. The moral law is not something away from the actuality of human life

【Text】

The moral law is not something away from the actuality of human life.

The Universal Order · Chapter XIII

【Commentary】

The moral law is around us, whose operation we cannot escape for one instant in our existence.

忠恕违道不远

Carrying out the principles of conscientiousness and reciprocity, he is not far from the moral law

17. 忠恕违道不远

【原文】

忠恕违道不远，施诸己而不愿，亦勿施于人。

《中庸·第十三章》

【释文】

一个人做到忠恕，离道也就不远了。所谓忠恕就是自己不愿意别人施加给自己的，也不要施加给别人。

【解析】

忠恕之道指的是推己及人，将心比心。正如孔子所说：自己想要在社会上立足也要让别人在社会上立足，自己想要事事通达也要让别人事事通达。自己所不想要的东西，不要强加在别人身上。以仁爱责己，以忠恕待人。

17. Carrying out the principles of conscientiousness and reciprocity, he is not far from the moral law

【Text】

When a man carries out the principles of conscientiousness and reciprocity, he is not far from the moral law. What you do not wish others should do unto you, do not do unto them.

The Universal Order · Chapter XIII

【Commentary】

The principles of conscientiousness and reciprocity require us to treat others as one expects to be treated and to think into others' minds. Just as Confucius once remarked, "A moral man in forming his character forms the character of others; in enlightening himself he enlightens others." What you do not wish others should do unto you, do not do unto them. Always be humane, caring, conscientious and tolerant.

18. 庸德之行，庸言之谨

【原文】

庸德之行，庸言之谨，有所不足，不敢不勉，有余不敢尽。

《中庸·第十三章》

【释文】

平常的德行努力去实践；平常的言谈则尽量谨慎；德行的践行有不足的地方，不敢不勤勉地去跟进；如有做得好的地方，在言谈时却不敢放肆而把话说尽。

【解析】

孔子曾说，君子做事要敏捷而说话要谨慎。

18. The discharge of the ordinary duties of life; the exercise of care in ordinary conversation

【Text】

In the discharge of the ordinary duties of life and in the exercise of care in ordinary conversation, whenever there is shortcoming, never fail to strive for improvement, and when there is much to be said, always say less than what is necessary.

The Universal Order · Chapter XIII

【Commentary】

Confucius remarked, "A wise man wants to be slow in speech and diligent in conduct."

言顾行，行顾言

Words having respect to actions; actions having respect to words

19. 言顾行，行顾言

【原文】

言顾行，行顾言，君子胡不慥慥尔！

《中庸·第十三章》

【释文】

言语要顾到自己的行为，行为也要顾到自己的言语，这样的君子怎么会是不忠厚笃实呢！

【解析】

言行一致是忠厚诚实的基本要求。

19. Words having respect to actions; actions having respect to words

【Text】

Words having respect to actions and actions having respect to words. Is it not just this thorough genuineness and absence of pretence which characterizes the moral man?

The Universal Order · Chapter XIII

【Commentary】

Matching words to actions is essential for thorough genuineness and absence of pretence.

20. 君子素其位而行

【原文】

君子素其位而行，不愿乎其外。

《中庸·第十四章》

【释文】

君子安处于现在所处的地位去做自己本位的事，不倾慕本位之外的东西。

【解析】

作为君子，无论在什么时候，在什么地方，处在什么地位上，总是从此时、此地、此位的实际出发，坚定地走在中正的道路上。

20. The moral man conforms himself to his life circumstances

【Text】

The moral man conforms himself to his life circumstances; he does not desire anything outside of his position.

The Universal Order · Chapter XIV

【Commentary】

A true moral man, regardless of the time, place and position, always proceeds from the reality and chooses the way of central balance.

正己而不求于人

The moral man puts in order his own personal conduct and seeks nothing from others

21. 正己而不求于人

【原文】

君子无入而不自得焉。在上位，不陵下；在下位，不援上。正己而不求于人则无怨。

《中庸·第十四章》

【释文】

君子无论处于什么情况都能安然自得。处在上位不欺侮在下位的人，处在下位不巴结在上位的人。端正自己而不苛求别人，这样就不会有什么怨恨了。

【解析】

这是君子待人接物最基本的态度和修养。孔子说：对自己责备得重而对别人则责备得轻，就可以远离别人的怨恨了。

21. The moral man puts in order his own personal conduct and seeks nothing from others

【Text】

The moral man can find himself in no situation in life in which he is not master of himself. In a high position, he does not domineer over his subordinates. In a subordinate position, he does not court the favors of his superiors. He puts in order his own personal conduct and seeks nothing from others; hence he has no complaint to make.

The Universal Order · Chapter XIV

【Commentary】

This line shows the attitudes and manners that a moral man must have in his conduct of life. Confucius remarked, "A man who expects much from himself and demands little from others will never have any enemies."

22. 上不怨天，下不尤人

【原文】

上不怨天，下不尤人。

《中庸·第十四章》

【释文】

上不抱怨天，下不抱怨人。

【解析】

孔子主张“不怨天，不尤人”，凡事首先要反省自己，从严要求自己。

22. He complains not against God nor rails against men

【Text】

He complains not against God nor rails against men.

The Universal Order · Chapter XIV

【Commentary】

Confucius thought one "should not complain against God nor rail against men." For anything he does, a moral man should reflect on his own faults and be strict with himself.

23. 君子居易以俟命

【原文】

故君子居易以俟命，小人行险以徼幸。

《中庸·第十四章》

【释文】

所以，君子安于平素的地位而等待天命的到来，小人却铤而走险妄图获得偶然的成功或意外地摆脱不幸。

【解析】

作为君子，总是秉持“求之有道，得之有命”（追求自己的人生目标自有一定的规律和原则，至于能否达到自有天命存在而不怨天尤人）的做人准则，朝着自己的人生目标做不懈的努力。至于道德卑下的小人，总是倾慕荣利，心存侥幸，企图通过歪门邪道，谋取私利，这是君子所不齿的。

23. The moral man lives out the even tenor of his life, calmly waiting for the appointment of God

【Text】

Thus it is that the moral man lives out the even tenor of his life, calmly waiting for the appointment of God, whereas the vulgar person takes to dangerous courses, expecting the uncertain chances of luck.

The Universal Order · Chapter XIV

【Commentary】

A moral man must follow a rule: when seeking, he must act according to the moral order; when acquiring, he must wait for the providential ordinance. A moral man should exert unremitting efforts toward what he aims to achieve in life. The vulgar persons, however, always aspire for fame and profits, and they gamble on uncertain chances of luck. They seek personal gains through crooked practices. This is what a moral man feels ashamed of.

君子反求诸其身

The moral man turns round and seeks for the cause of his failure within himself

24. 君子反求诸其身

【原文】

射有似乎君子，失诸正鹄，反求诸其身。

《中庸·第十四章》

【释文】

射箭与君子立身处世有相似之处，射不中箭靶的中心就反省自己，从自己身上找原因。

【解析】

只有真诚反省，才能战胜困难，继续前进。

24. The moral man turns round and seeks for the cause of his failure within himself

【Text】

In the practice of archery we have something resembling the principle in a moral man's life. When the archer misses the centre of the target, he turns round and seeks for the cause of his failure within himself.

The Universal Order · Chapter XIV

【Commentary】

Only when a man sincerely reflects on his own faults could he overcome the difficulties and move forward.

行远必自迩，登高必自卑

Start from the nearest stage when traveling afar;
begin from the lowest step while ascending a height

25. 行远必自迩，登高必自卑

【原文】

君子之道，辟如行远，必自迩；辟如登高，必自卑。

《中庸·第十五章》

【释文】

君子实行中庸之道，就像走远路一样，一定要从近处开始；就像登高山一样，一定要从低处起步。

【解析】

君子修道，当从近处做起，从小事做起，从今日做起。

25. Start from the nearest stage when traveling afar; begin from the lowest step while ascending a height

【Text】

The moral life of man may be likened to travelling to a distant place: one must start from the nearest stage. It may also be likened to ascending a height: one must begin from the lowest step.

The Universal Order · Chapter XV

【Commentary】

To lead a moral life, a man should start from doing small things, right now and right here.

26. 诚之不可掩

【原文】

夫微之显，诚之不可掩如此夫！

《中庸·第十六章》

【释文】

从鬼神般的隐微之处出发而造成显著的功德，真诚专一的心就是这样不可掩盖啊！

【解析】

这里所说的“鬼神”，是用来说明“道”的功效的神奇、微妙和无所不在。只要真诚专一，信仰执着，就能一步步走向成功。

26. It is impossible to doubt the spiritual nature of man

【Text】

Such is the evidence of things invisible that it is impossible to doubt the spiritual nature of man.

The Universal Order · Chapter XVI

【Commentary】

This line shows how wonderful, delicate and omnipresent the moral order is! With a sincere heart and a firm belief, a single-minded and persistent person can gradually achieve success.

大德必得其位

He who possesses great moral qualities will certainly attain to corresponding high position

27. 大德必得其位

【原文】

大德必得其位，必得其禄，必得其名，必得其寿。

《中庸·第十七章》

【释文】

有大德的人必定得到他应得的尊贵地位，必定得到他应得的丰厚财富，必定得到他应得的美好名声，必定得到他应得的永年高寿。

【解析】

这里所表达的是一种“圣贤政治观”：只有圣贤才能受天命，换句话说，受天命者必须是圣贤。这种观念对无德的暴君是一种批判，对君主世袭制观念也是一种有力的冲击。

27. He who possesses great moral qualities will certainly attain to corresponding high position

【Text】

Thus it is that he who possesses great moral qualities will certainly attain to corresponding high position; to corresponding great prosperity; to corresponding great name; to corresponding great age.

The Universal Order · Chapter XVII

【Commentary】

This line expresses a political view of the sages and the worthiness in ancient times: Only the sages and the worthiness deserve the appointment of the providential ordinance. In other words, he who receives the providential appointment must be a man with perfect nature or a worthy man. This point of view is indirectly critical of the worthless tyrant. It is also forcefully against the hereditary monarchy.

28. 天之生物，必因其材而笃焉

【原文】

天之生物，必因其材而笃焉。故栽者培之，倾者覆之。

《中庸·第十七章》

【释文】

所以上天生养万物，必定根据它们的资质而厚待它们。能栽培成材的就得到培育生长，歪斜不能成材的就让它倒伏灭亡。

【解析】

社会的大厦，需要栋梁支撑。立志成才者终究会得到认可与扶持，成为栋梁之材。而自暴自弃者，则必将被时代所抛弃。

28. For God in giving life to all created things is surely bountiful to them according to their qualities

【Text】

For God in giving life to all created things is surely bountiful to them according to their qualities. Hence the tree that is full of life, he fosters and sustains, while that which is ready to fall, he cuts off and destroys.

The Universal Order · Chapter XVII

【Commentary】

To establish an edifice, giant pillars are needed. Those with great expectation will be recognized and supported eventually, and thus become the pillars for the society. Those who abandon themselves to despair will in turn be abandoned by the time.

29. 大德者必受命

【原文】

大德者必受命。

《中庸·第十七章》

【释文】

有大德的人必定会承受天命。

【解析】

有理想有抱负的人，应自觉地承担“治国平天下”的历史使命。

29. He who possesses exceedingly great moral qualities will certainly receive the divine call to the Imperial throne

【Text】

It is therefore true that he who possesses exceedingly great moral qualities will certainly receive the divine call to the Imperial throne.

The Universal Order · Chapter XVII

【Commentary】

Those with great ambition and expectation should carry out consciously the historical mission of "securing a good government and bringing peace to the world."

父作之，子述之

His father laid the foundation of his House and his son carried it on

周

30. 父作之，子述之

【原文】

无忧者其惟文王乎！……父作之，子述之。

《中庸·第十八章》

【释文】

古来帝王无忧的大概只有周文王吧！……父亲王季为他开创了基业，儿子武王继承了他的遗志，完成了他所没有完成的事业。

【解析】

武王伐纣，以周代殷，这是上古史上一件惊天动地的大事。此一大事，文王奠其基，武王建其功，周公助其成。殷周之际，不但有此政治上的大变动，在思想观念上也是巨大的变革。殷人尊天事鬼，如按旧的天命观，武王伐纣，是以下犯上，大逆不道。但周人敬德保民，认为伐纣之举是“顺天应人”。周人尚德，就是重道，并以伐纣灭殷之大业证明了道用之广大，足以用来建立旷世之伟业。

30. His father laid the foundation of his House and his son carried it on

【Text】

The man perhaps who enjoyed the most perfect happiness was the Emperor Wen. His father laid the foundation of his House and his son carried it on.

The Universal Order · Chapter XVIII

【Commentary】

Emperor Wu led his troops to attack Emperor Zhou, and replaced the Yin Dynasty with the Zhou Dynasty. This was an epoch-making event. Emperor Wen laid the foundation of his House, and Emperor Wu, with the assistance of Duke Zhou, established his own empire. During that transitional period, there were great changes in both political systems and ideological thoughts. People in the Yin Dynasty respected the heaven and worshiped the ghosts. From the old perspective on heaven and fate, Emperor Wu's attacking was treacherous. But people in the Zhou Dynasty valued the moral nature and social benefits, therefore, they deemed that the heroic action was carried out "in accordance with the providential ordinance and people's requests." During the period of the Zhou, its rulers put a high value on moral nature. This historical event demonstrates that the moral order is so universally applicable that even the great political cause could be realized by adhering to it.

夫孝者，善继人之志，善述人之事

True filial piety consists in carrying out the unfinished work of our forefathers and transmitting their achievements to posterity

31. 夫孝者，善继人之志，善述人之事

【原文】

夫孝者，善继人之志，善述人之事者也。

《中庸·第十九章》

【释文】

所谓孝的最高境界，就是要（像周武王和周公那样）善于继承前人的遗志，善于完成前人所未完成的事业。

【解析】

武王继承文王遗志，伐纣灭殷，建立周王朝。武王死后，周公辅佐成王，东征平叛，分封诸侯，制礼作乐，天下大治，又一次证明了道用之广大。周公制礼作乐，是围绕着宗法制进行的。在当时，实行分封制、宗法制，对巩固王权，促进统一，维护社会稳定，恢复和发展生产，具有进步意义和积极作用。而周公的制礼作乐，则是围绕着宗法制，建立起一系列的社会、政治制度，以及与之适应的一系列的道德伦理规范和文化教育制度。这是当时社会进一步走向文明的重要标志。

31. True filial piety consists in carrying out the unfinished work of our forefathers and transmitting their achievements to posterity

【Text】

Now, true filial piety consists in successfully carrying out the unfinished work of our forefathers and transmitting their achievements to posterity.

The Universal Order · Chapter XIX

【Commentary】

Emperor Wu carried out the unfinished work of his father Emperor Wen, and overthrew Emperor Zhou of the Yin Dynasty and established the Zhou Dynasty. After Emperor Wu's death, Emperor Cheng, assisted by Duke Zhou, put down the rebellion in the east, granted the titles and territories to the nobles, recreated the ceremonial rituals and music, and furthered the cause of peace and prosperity, all of which demonstrated the moral order is universally applicable. At that time, the establishment of patriarchal clan system and the enfeoffment system were of great historical significance, because it played an active role in consolidating the monarchy, promoting reunification, maintaining social stability, restoring and developing production, etc.. Based on patriarchal clan system, Duke Zhou drew up the ceremonial rites and music, and set up a series of social and political systems, ethical regulations, cultural and educational systems. This was an important sign that a more civilized society was being formed.

32. 人存政举，人亡政息

【原文】

文武之政，布在方策。其人存，则其政举；其人亡，则其政息。

《中庸·第二十章》

【释文】

周文王、周武王的政事都记载在典籍上。今天如果像文王、武王那样的人在世，这些政事就能实施；今天如果没有像文王、武王那样的人在世，这些政事也就息灭了。

【解析】

今天我们致力于建设法治国家，但“法”毕竟要通过“人”来制定和施行。因此提高人的素质，是建设法治国家必不可少的条件。孔子高度重视“人”的因素，认为“为政在人”，要治理好天下国家，关键在执政者本人的素质。因而执政者本人应以修身为本。

32. When the men are there, good government will flourish, but when the men are gone, good government decays and becomes extinct

【Text】

The principles of good government of the Emperors Wen and Wu are abundantly illustrated in the records preserved. When the men are there, good government will flourish, but when the men are gone, good government decays and becomes extinct.

The Universal Order · Chapter XX

【Commentary】

Today we Chinese people work hard to build a country by law, yet it is the "human beings" who will draw up and carry out the "law." Therefore, self-improvement is indispensable for this cause. Confucius attached great importance to "human beings," and he thought that whether a good government will flourish or not lies in the rulers themselves. Thus men in authority should take self-cultivation as the foundation of their political careers.

33. 人道敏政，地道敏树

【原文】

人道敏政，地道敏树。

《中庸·第二十章》

【释文】

治理人的正道是勤于政事，治理地的正道是勤种庄稼。

【解析】

只有勤政，才能建功。

33. With the right men the growth of good government is as rapid as the growth of vegetation is in the right soil

【Text】

With the right men the growth of good government is as rapid as the growth of vegetation is in the right soil.

The Universal Order · Chapter XX

【Commentary】

A man of great industry will guarantee the achievements in his political performance.

仁者人也，义者宜也

The moral sense is the characteristic attribute of man;
the sense of justice is the recognition of what is right and proper

34. 仁者人也，义者宜也

【原文】

仁者，人也，亲亲为大。义者，宜也，尊贤为大。

《中庸·第二十章》

【释文】

仁就是爱人，亲爱自己的亲人是最根本的仁。义就是事事做得适宜，尊重贤人是最重要的义。

【解析】

儒家认为，孝悌是仁德的根本，由孝悌可以拓展为忠恕与爱民。儒家又认为，仁是心，义是路，君子当“居仁由义”，推行贤能政治，就是实现社会公平正义最重要的保证。

34. The moral sense is the characteristic attribute of man; the sense of justice is the recognition of what is right and proper

【Text】

The moral sense is the characteristic attribute of man. To feel natural affection for those nearly related to us is the highest expression of the moral sense. The sense of justice is the recognition of what is right and proper. To honor those who are worthier than ourselves is the highest expression of the sense of justice.

The Universal Order · Chapter XX

【Commentary】

Confucius remarked, "Now, to be a good son and a good citizen—do not these form the foundation of a moral life?" And filial piety can be developed into loyalty, charity and love for people. According to Confucianism, humanity (the moral sense) can be likened to the heart, and honor (the sense of justice) can be likened to the path. A moral man should "abide in humanity and by honor." To promote the talents is vital to realize social justice and fairness.

35. 天下之五达道

【原文】

君臣也，父子也，夫妇也，昆弟也，朋友之交也；五者，天下之达道也。

《中庸·第二十章》

【释文】

君臣、父子、夫妇、兄弟、朋友之间的交往，这五项是天下人普遍的伦常关系。

【解析】

儒家主张父慈子孝，兄友弟恭，君臣相得，夫妻相敬，朋友有信，认为这是社会上最普遍的伦理道德。

35. The five duties of universal obligation

【Text】

The duties are those between ruler and subject; between father and son; between husband and wife; between elder brother and younger; and those in the intercourse between friends. These are the five duties of universal obligation.

The Universal Order · Chapter XX

【Commentary】

Confucius remarked, a good father loves his children and a good son honors his father; the elder and the younger brothers should always be earnest to each other; let the ruler treat his subject with honor and the subject serve the ruler with loyalty; the husband and wife should always maintain the same careful respect; in the intercourse with friends, he should always be sincere and truthful. These are the moral duties of universal obligation.

天下之三达德

The three universally recognized moral qualities of man

趙

36. 天下之三达德

【原文】

知、仁、勇三者，天下之达德也，所以行之者一也。

《中庸·第二十章》

【释文】

智、仁、勇这三种道德，是天下人用来处理这五项伦常关系的德行，至于这三种德行的实施，道理都是一样的。

【解析】

孔子说：聪明的人不会被迷惑，有仁德的人没有忧虑，勇敢的人无所畏惧。

36. The three universally recognized moral qualities of man

【Text】

Intelligence, moral character and courage: these are the three universally recognized moral qualities of man. It matters not in what way men come to the exercise of these moral qualities, the result is one and the same.

The Universal Order · Chapter XX

【Commentary】

Confucius remarked, "Men of intelligence are free from doubts, moral men from anxiety, and men of courage from fear."

37. 好学近乎知，力行近乎仁，知耻近乎勇

【原文】

好学近乎知，力行近乎仁，知耻近乎勇。

《中庸·第二十章》

【释文】

喜欢学习就接近了智，努力实行就接近了仁，知道羞耻就接近了勇。

【解析】

这里进一步指明了完善“三达德”的具体途径。

37. Love of knowledge is the characteristic of men of intellectual character; strenuous attention to conduct is the characteristic of men of moral character; sensitiveness to shame is the characteristic of men of courage

【Text】

Love of knowledge is the characteristic of men of intellectual character. Strenuous attention to conduct is the characteristic of men of moral character. Sensitiveness to shame is the characteristic of men of courage or heroic character.

The Universal Order · Chapter XX

【Commentary】

These are the specific approaches through which men come to exercise the three universally recognized moral qualities.

凡为天下国家有九经

Nine cardinal directions for every government of nations and empires

38. 凡为天下国家有九经

【原文】

凡为天下国家有九经，曰：修身也，尊贤也，亲亲也，敬大臣也，体群臣也，子庶民也，来百工也，柔远人也，怀诸侯也。

《中庸·第二十章》

【释文】

大凡治理天下和国家有九条常道。那就是：修养自身，尊重贤人，亲爱亲人，礼敬大臣，体恤群臣，爱民如子，招纳工匠，优待远客，安抚诸侯。

【解析】

这九条常道是以“修身”为根本出发点。孔子主张：修养自己，使自己严肃恭敬；修养自己，使别人安乐；修养自己，使天下所有老百姓都安乐。

38. Nine cardinal directions for every government of nations and empires

【Text】

For every one called to the government of nations and empires there are nine cardinal directions to be attended to:

1. Putting in order his personal conduct.

2. Honoring worthy men.

3. Cherishing affection for, and doing his duty towards, his kindred.

4. Showing respect to the high ministers of state.

5. Identifying himself with the interests and welfare of the whole body of public officers.

6. Showing himself as a father to the common people.

7. Encouraging the introduction of all useful arts.

8. Showing tenderness to strangers from far countries.

9. Taking interest in the welfare of the princes of the Empire.

The Universal Order · Chapter XX

【Commentary】

These nine cardinal directions serve as a starting point for self-cultivation. Confucius remarked, "A wise and good man is one who sets himself seriously to order his conversation aright. He wants to order his conversation aright for the happiness of others. He wants to order his conversation aright for the happiness of the world."

凡事豫则立，不豫则废

Success depends on preparation in all matters,
without which there will always be failure

39. 凡事豫则立，不豫则废

【原文】

凡事豫则立，不豫则废。

《中庸·第二十章》

【释文】

任何事情，事先有预备就会成功，没有预备就会失败。

【解析】

做任何事情都要预先规划。尤其是治理国家，一定要有明确的目标，长远的规划，要预先制订出切实可行的措施。

39. Success depends on preparation in all matters, without which there will always be failure

【Text】

In all matters, success depends on preparation; without preparation there will always be failure.

The Universal Order · Chapter XX

【Commentary】

Preparation is needed in all matters. In particular, it is important for the rulers to have clear objectives and long-term plans. Realistic measures should be formulated in advance.

40. 诚者天之道，诚之者人之道

【原文】

诚者，天之道也；诚之者，人之道也。

《中庸·第二十章》

【释文】

真诚是上天的原则，追求真诚是做人的原则。

【解析】

所谓“人之诚”，就是真诚无妄，专一不二，恪守中道，谨言慎行。人如能保持“从容中道”的本性，就是“善”，就与天道相符合，达到“天人合一”。

40. Truth is the law of God; acquired truth is the law of man

【Text】

Truth is the law of God. Acquired truth is the law of man.

The Universal Order · Chapter XX

【Commentary】

By "truth," it denotes the sincere attribute of human character. One must scrupulously observe the moral order in one's thinking and action, taking the appropriate measure at a sedate pace. As long as a man acts in line with the moral order, "the harmony of man with nature" can be achieved, for maintaining the central point in one's moral being meets the requirement of "good conduct."

诚之者，择善而固执

He who acquires truth is one who finds out what is good and holds fast to it

41. 诚之者，择善而固执

【原文】

诚者，不勉而中，不思而得，从容中道，圣人也。诚之者，择善而固执之者也：博学之，审问之，慎思之，明辨之，笃行之。

《中庸·第二十章》

【释文】

天生真诚的人，不用勉强就能做到，不用思考就能拥有，从容不迫地走在中庸的大道上，这样的人就是圣人。努力做到真诚，就要选择“善”并执着地追求：广泛地学习，详细地询问，周密地思考，明确地分辨，切实地实行。

【解析】

人一旦认定了“善”的目标或理想，就要一心一意全力以赴去追求，这就叫作“择善而固执”。至于如何“择善”，则要在博学、审问、慎思、明辨的基础上，明确认定了“善”的目标或理想，然后“笃行之”，诚心去追求，力求它的实现。孔子论“诚”，实际上是论人的信仰和追求，也就是对中庸之道的信仰和追求。

41. He who acquires truth is one who finds out what is good and holds fast to it

【Text】

He who intuitively apprehends truth is one who, with effort, hits what is right and without thinking, understands what he wants to know; whose life easily and naturally is in harmony with the moral law. Such a one is what we call a saint or a man of divine nature. He who acquires truth is one who finds out what is good and holds fast to it. In order to acquire truth, it is necessary to obtain a wide and expensive knowledge of what has been said and done in the world; to critically inquire into it; to carefully ponder over it; to clearly sift it; and earnestly carry it out.

The Universal Order · Chapter XX

【Commentary】

As long as a "good" goal is fixed, one must exert all possible efforts to achieve it, and that is "finding out what is good and holding fast to it." As to "finding out what is good," one needs to obtain an expensive knowledge of what has been said and done in the world; to critically inquire into it; to carefully ponder over it; to clearly sift it; and earnestly carry it out. One must make every endeavor to fulfill the task. The "absolute truth" that Confucius discussed is what human beings are seeking as a religion: the universal moral order.

42. 人一能之己百之，人十能之己千之

【原文】

人一能之，己百之；人十能之，己千之。果能此道矣，虽愚必明，虽柔必强。

《中庸·第二十章》

【释文】

别人用一分努力就能做到的，我用一百分的努力去做；别人用十分的努力做到的，我用一千分的努力去做。如果真能够做到这样，虽然愚笨也一定可以聪明起来，虽然柔弱也一定可以刚强起来。

【解析】

对理想的追求，需要决心和毅力，有时可能需要付出较之常人百倍千倍的努力。

42. If another man succeeds by one effort, you will use a hundred efforts

【Text】

If another man succeeds by one effort, you will use a hundred efforts. If another man succeeds by ten efforts, you will use a thousand efforts. Let a man really proceed in this manner, and, though dull, he will surely become intelligent; though weak, he will surely become strong.

The Universal Order · Chapter XX

【Commentary】

In order to achieve success, one needs determination and persistence. Sometimes, one needs to exert a hundred or even a thousand efforts to win in the competition.

自诚明谓之性，自明诚谓之教

The intuition and education

知先行後

43. 自诚明谓之性，自明诚谓之教

【原文】

自诚明，谓之性；自明诚，谓之教。

《中庸·第二十一章》

【释文】

由于内心真诚而自然明白道理，这叫作天赋的本性；由明白道理后做到真诚，这叫作后天人为的教化。

【解析】

子思认为，圣人内心诚实而领会了中庸之道，明确了事理，这是他先天具有的本性。一般人通过学习领会了中庸之道，明确了事理，这是后天教育的结果。天赋的真诚本性固然可贵，后天的教化修养也同样重要。

43. The intuition and education

【Text】

The intelligence which comes from the direct apprehension of truth is intuition. The apprehension of truth which comes from the exercise of intelligence is the result of education.

The Universal Order · Chapter XXI

【Commentary】

According to Zisi, the fact that ancient men with perfect divine nature were able to understand the universal moral order and possess the absolute truth is because of their intuition. And the reason why we commoners are also able to do the same is because of the education. Thus, education and self-cultivation are as important as intuition.

44. 诚则明矣，明则诚矣

【原文】

诚则明矣，明则诚矣。

《中庸·第二十一章》

【释文】

内心真诚也就会自然明白道理，明白道理后也就会做到内心真诚。

【解析】

内心诚实与明确事理两者是相互为用的。内心诚实就可以日渐明确事理，而日渐明确事理又可使内心日益诚实。可知偏执绝非真正的信仰，而信仰也绝非愚昧的盲从。

44. The truth and intelligence

【Text】

Where there is truth, there is intelligence; where there is intelligence, there is truth.

The Universal Order · Chapter XXI

【Commentary】

The possession of truth and that of intelligence are interrelated to and interative with each other. The acquirement of truth prepares a more intelligent mind; and a more intelligent mind facilitates the acquirement of truth. Therefore, to believe in something is not to hold a paranoid idea, nor to fatuously or blindly conform to anything.

45. 唯天下至诚，可以赞天地之化育

【原文】

唯天下至诚，为能尽其性；能尽其性，则能尽人之性；能尽人之性，则能尽物之性；能尽物之性，则可以赞天地之化育；可以赞天地之化育，则可以与天地参矣。

《中庸·第二十二章》

【释文】

只有天下最真诚的圣人能充分发挥天赋的本性；能充分发挥天赋的本性，就能充分发挥众人的本性；能充分发挥众人的本性，就能充分发挥万物的本性；能充分发挥万物的本性，就可以帮助天地化育万物；能帮助天地化育万物，就可以与天地并列为三了。

【解析】

子思认为，只有天下至诚的圣人，最能发挥其天性，做到真诚无妄，从容中道，择善固执，遵道而行。他们也能让天下之人都发挥其本然的善性，从而使天下之物也能发挥其本然的善性，使天下万物顺利生长、蓬勃发展。这样一来，人就可以参与天地的化育，人与天地就可以并列为三了。也就是说，“人”取得了与“天地”并立的崇高地位。

45. He who possesses absolute truth can influence the forces of creation of the Universe

【Text】

It is only he, in the world, who possesses absolute truth who can get to the bottom of the law of his being. He who is able to get to the bottom of the law of his being will be able to get to the bottom of the law of being of other men. He who is able to get to the bottom of the law of being of men will be able to get to the bottom of the laws of physical nature. He who is able to get to the bottom of the laws of physical nature will be able to influence the forces of creation of the Universe. He who can influence the forces of creation of the Universe is one with the Powers of the Universe.

The Universal Order · Chapter XXII

【Commentary】

According to Zisi, only those who possess absolute truth can give full play to their endowed nature. Thus they are sincere and truthful; they maintain the central balance in their moral being; they choose what is good and hold fast to it; they act in accordance with the universal moral order. They are able to get to the bottom of the law of being of other men and the laws of physical nature. Therefore, he is able to influence the forces of creation of the universe. In this way, mankind is elevated to a position as important as the heaven and the earth.

唯天下至诚为能化

It is only he who possesses absolute truth in the world who can create

王陽明

46. 唯天下至诚为能化

【原文】

唯天下至诚为能化。

《中庸·第二十三章》

【释文】

只有天下最真诚的人才能化育万物。

【解析】

子思认为，那些次于圣人的贤人，可以通过一次又一次地学习和研究一个又一个具体而微的事物，领会真诚无妄的天道，从少到多，由小至大，自近及远，持之以恒，不断感动人心，同行中道，同样可以参与天地的化育，不是说只有圣人才可以参与天地的化育。

46. It is only he who possesses absolute truth in the world who can create

【Text】

It is only he who possesses absolute truth in the world who can create.

The Universal Order · Chapter XXIII

【Commentary】

According to Zisi, those worthy men are able to understand the laws of creation of the universe through studies on matters in the minutest details. In their persistent pursuit of truth, these worthy men will acquire more knowledge and maintain the central point in their moral being. They, like the ancient sages, can also influence the forces of creation of the Universe.

47. 至诚之道，可以前知

【原文】

至诚之道，可以前知。

《中庸·第二十四章》

【释文】

极端真诚可以预知未来的事。

【解析】

为什么掌握了“至诚之道”，就可以预见未来呢？因为至诚之道就是中庸之道。子思认为，国家的发展如果遵循中庸之道而行，则必兴盛，如果违背中庸之道而行，必然会出现种种奇怪现象、非常现象，最后导致国家灭亡。这种“至诚之道”（也就是中庸之道），像一块试金石，用来观察现实、掌握国家走向是十分灵验的。

47. It is an attribute of the possession of absolute truth to be able to foreknow

【Text】

It is an attribute of the possession of absolute truth to be able to foreknow.

The Universal Order · Chapter XXIV

【Commentary】

Why is a man who possesses the absolute truth able to foreknow? Because the absolute truth is the universal moral order. According to Zisi, a nation will flourish if its rulers act in line with the universal moral order; or else, there will be ill omens and uncommon signs, and a nation will fall. The absolute truth is the touchstone of a nation's future.

国家将兴，必有祯祥

When a nation or family is about to flourish,
there are sure to be lucky omens

48. 国家将兴，必有祯祥

【原文】

国家将兴，必有祯祥；国家将亡，必有妖孽。

《中庸·第二十四章》

【释文】

国家将要兴旺，一定会有吉祥的征兆；国家将要衰亡，一定会有不祥的反常现象。

【解析】

国家兴衰，都会有先兆。因此，执政者要“知几”（几：苗头，征兆）。知几，就是要见几而作，抢占先机，或防微杜渐，让问题消灭在萌芽状态。

48. When a nation or family is about to flourish, there are sure to be lucky omens

【Text】

When a nation or family is about to flourish, there are sure to be lucky omens. When a nation or family is about to perish, there are sure to be signs and prodigies.

The Universal Order · Chapter XXIV

【Commentary】

There will be omens for the rise or the fall of a nation. Therefore, men in authority must be able to "tell the symptom of a trend," and take proactive measures to nip the vice in the bud.

49. 至诚如神

【原文】

祸福将至，善，必先知之，不善，必先知之。故至诚如神。

《中庸·第二十四章》

【释文】

祸福将要来临时，是福一定可以预先知道，是祸也一定可以预先知道。所以极端真诚就像神灵一样神奇微妙可以预知未来。

【解析】

有了极端真诚的信仰和追求，就能保持清醒的头脑，作出正确的判断，从而采取措施，积极应对。

49. He who possesses absolute truth is like a spiritual being

【Text】

When happiness or calamity is about to come, it can be known beforehand. When it is good, it can be known beforehand. When it is evil, it can also be known beforehand. Therefore he who possesses absolute truth is like a spiritual being.

The Universal Order · Chapter XXIV

【Commentary】

If you go for what you believe in with an extremely sincere attitude, you are then able to keep a clear mind, make correct judgment, and take active measures to deal with the problems.

君子诚之为贵

The moral man values truth

50. 君子诚之为贵

【原文】

诚者，自成也；而道，自道也。诚者，物之终始，不诚无物。是故君子诚之为贵。

《中庸·第二十五章》

【释文】

真诚，就是成全自我、完善道德的重要准则。而大道，则是引导自我走向道德完善的道路。真诚既是万物的发端也是万物的归宿，没有真诚就没有万物。因此君子以真诚为贵。

【解析】

真诚无妄的“诚”，是人自己主动修养而形成的品德，中庸之道的“道”，是人自己主动抉择而选定的道路。因此，人们应以“诚”为贵。

50. The moral man values truth

【Text】

Truth means the realization of our being; and moral law means the law of our being. Truth is the beginning and end of existence. Without truth there is no existence. It is for this reason that the moral man values truth.

The Universal Order · Chapter XXV

【Commentary】

"Truth" is a moral character nurtured and developed through a moral man's own efforts; "moral law" found in the universal moral order can be likened to a path that a moral man chooses to take. Thus, we should value truth.

诚者，既成己又成物

Truth is the realization of our own being;
it is also that by which things outside of us have an existence

51. 诚者，既成己又成物

【原文】

诚者，非自成己而已也，所以成物也。

《中庸·第二十五章》

【释文】

真诚并不是自我完善就够了，而是还要完善万物。

【解析】

对“至诚之道”（也就是中庸之道）的信仰和追求，既“成己”（修身），又“成物”（齐家治国平天下），两者是紧密联系在一起的。

51. Truth is the realization of our own being; it is also that by which things outside of us have an existence

【Text】

Truth is not only the realization of our own being: it is that by which things outside of us have an existence.

The Universal Order · Chapter XXV

【Commentary】

The pursuit of "the absolute truth" will not only bring about the realization of our own being, but also will help fulfill the tasks of putting the house in order, securing a good government and furthering the cause of civilization in the world, because these two aspects are highly relevant.

52. 成己仁也，成物知也

【原文】

成己，仁也；成物，知也。性之德也，合外内之道也，故时措之宜也。

《中庸·第二十五章》

【释文】

自我完善是“仁”，完善万物是“智”。“仁”和“智”是出于人的本性中固有的美德，是融合自身与外物既“成己”又“成物”的普遍准则，所以任何时候施行都是适宜的。

【解析】

能“成己”，叫作“仁”；能“成物”，叫作“智”。这些都应是人本性中固有的东西。把向内以“成己”的“仁”与向外以“成物”的“智”结合起来，就是人生的正道，那是“放之四海而皆准”的普遍真理。

52. The realization of our being is moral sense; the realization of things outside of us is intellect

【Text】

The realization of our being is moral sense. The realization of things outside of us is intellect. These, moral sense and intellect, are the powers or faculties of our being. They combine the inner or subjective and outer or objective use of the power of the mind. Therefore with truth everything done is right.

The Universal Order · Chapter XXV

【Commentary】

Both the "moral sense" and the "intellect" are intrinsic character of human nature. Only when the internal "moral sense" and the external "intellect" are combined can we acquire the absolute truth that is "universally applicable."

至诚无息

The absolute truth is indestructible

53. 至诚无息

【原文】

故至诚无息，不息则久，久则征，征则悠远，悠远则博厚，博厚则高明。博厚，所以载物也；高明，所以覆物也；悠久，所以成物也。博厚配地，高明配天，悠久无疆。

《中庸·第二十六章》

【释文】

因此，极端真诚是没有止息的，没有止息就会保持长久，保持长久就会显露征信，显露征信就会悠远无尽，悠远无尽就会广博深厚，广博深厚就会高大光明。广博深厚，就可以承载万物；高大光明，就可以覆盖万物；悠远无尽，就可以生成万物。广博深厚可以与地相比，高大光明可以与天相比，悠远无尽则是永无止境。

【解析】

至诚之道也就是天地之道。天地是诚一不贰、纯粹精微的。所以天总是那么高明，无所不覆，地总是那么广博，无所不载。人效法天地至诚之道，执中守正，折中致和，终身奉行，永不停息，那么万物就会蓬勃发育生长。

53. The absolute truth is indestructible

【Text】

Thus absolute truth is indestructible. Being indestructible, it is eternal. Being eternal, it is self-existent. Being self-existent, it is infinite. Being infinite, it is vast and deep. Being vast and deep, it is transcendental and intelligent. It is because it is vast and deep that it contains all existence. It is because it is transcendental and intelligent that it embraces all existence. It is because it is infinite and eternal that it fills all existence. In vastness and depth it is like the Earth. In transcendental intelligence it is like Heaven. Infinite and eternal, it is Infinitude itself.

The Universal Order · Chapter XXVI

【Commentary】

The absolute truth denotes the universal moral order. The universe, or the heaven and the earth, is true and pure. Being transcendental and intelligent, the heaven embraces all existence. Being vast and deep, the earth contains all existence. Human beings should observe the universal order, maintain the central point and guard the upright, keep the central balance and fulfill the moral sense, and hold fast to the universal law, so that all existence in the universe will flourish.

54. 极高明而道中庸

【原文】

君子尊德性而道问学，致广大而尽精微，极高明而道中庸。

《中庸·第二十七章》

【释文】

君子诚心尊崇天赋的德性也努力从事后天的学习，广泛追求极其广博的知识也深入钻研极其精微的学问，达到极其高明的境界也遵循不偏不倚的中庸之道。

【解析】

圣人能效法天道，参与天地的化育。君子就应以圣人为榜样，尊重那天赋的德性而又努力问道求学，使学问既广博又精深，诚心诚意遵循中庸之道而行，从而达到最高明的境界。

54. Seek to understand the highest things, and live a plain, ordinary life in accordance with the moral order

【Text】

Wherefore the moral man, while honoring the greatness and power of his moral nature, yet does not neglect inquiry and pursuit of knowledge. While widening the extent of his knowledge, he yet seeks to attain utmost accuracy in the minutest details. While seeking to understand the highest things, he yet lives a plain, ordinary life in accordance with the moral order.

The Universal Order · Chapter XXVII

【Commentary】

The ancient men with perfect nature followed the universal order and influenced the forces of creation of the universe. A moral man should take the sages as role models and depend on both intuition and education, so that he could widen the extent of his knowledge and attain the utmost accuracy in the minutest details. As long as he acts in accordance with the universal moral order, he will reach the realm of the highest excellence.

温故而知新，敦厚以崇礼

Going over what he has already acquired,
he keeps adding to it new knowledge

55. 温故而知新，敦厚以崇礼

【原文】

温故而知新，敦厚以崇礼。

《中庸·第二十七章》

【释文】

温习已有的知识从而获得新知识，以道德的淳厚来崇奉礼仪法度。

【解析】

温习历史，继承传统，是为了获取新知，开创未来。修养身心，增强道德，是为了修明法度，治国安邦。

55. Going over what he has already acquired, he keeps adding to it new knowledge

【Text】

Going over what he has already acquired, he keeps adding to it new knowledge. Earnest and simple, he respects and obeys the laws and usages of social life.

The Universal Order · Chapter XXVII

【Commentary】

To acquire new knowledge and make achievements in future, we need to draw experience from the history and carry on the tradition. To formulate impartial laws and secure a good government, we need to nurture and cultivate our body and the mind, so as to improve our moral standards.

56. 愚而好自用，贱而好自专，灾必及其身

【原文】

愚而好自用；贱而好自专；生乎今之世，反古之道。如此者，灾及其身者也。

《中庸·第二十八章》

【释文】

愚昧的人却往往喜欢凭自己主观想法行事，卑贱的人却往往喜欢独断专行，生于当今之世，却一心想恢复古代的礼制。这样做，灾祸一定会降临到自己的身上。

【解析】

持守中庸之道，必须依礼而行，切勿“自用”“自专”，随心所欲，自以为是，离开中庸之道，走向极端与偏执。但礼不是一成不变的，每一时代的礼相对于前代都会有所损益，盲目复古只会适得其反。礼的核心是制度和秩序，是人人必须遵守的社会行为规范，其功能是调节人与人之间的关系。礼的作用，以保持中道与和谐为可贵。儒家所说的“礼”实为中庸之道的具体体现。

56. He who is foolish and fond of using his own judgment will bring calamity upon himself

【Text】

A man who is foolish, and yet is fond of using his own judgment; who is in humble circumstances, and yet is fond of assuming authority; who, while living in the present age, reverts to the ways of antiquity: such a man is one who will bring calamity upon himself.

The Universal Order · Chapter XXVIII

【Commentary】

A man should maintain the universal moral order and act in accordance with rituals. He should not be fond of "using his own judgment, or assuming authority." Otherwise, he will depart from the universal order and go to the extremes. However, rituals are not static. Ceremonial rituals and usages of social life during a period of time have both merits and demerits, compared with those in the previous dynasties. Thus only the opposite result will be achieved if we blindly follow suit. In essence, rituals are about institutions and orders, as well as the codes of conducts that each and everyone in the society should abide by. Rituals aim to regulate interpersonal relationships. It is essential that the universal order and harmony are maintained with the aid of rituals. The "rituals" in Confucianism are in fact embodiments of the universal moral order.

57. 君子之道百世以俟圣人而不惑

【原文】

君子之道，本诸身，征诸庶民，考诸三王而不缪，建诸天地而不悖，质诸鬼神而无疑，百世以俟圣人而不惑。

《中庸·第二十九章》

【释文】

君子治理天下应该以自身的品德为根本，并通过实践从老百姓那里得到验证，考察夏、商、周三代先王的做法而没有背谬，立于天地之间而没有悖乱，质询于鬼神而没有疑问，百世以后待圣人出现也没有什么迷惑不解的地方。

【解析】

君子处在上位，当谨慎行事，一切依中道而行。行事要根据并符合自身的修养和地位，要考虑民众的反映和诉求，要吸取历史的经验，要能经受住验证，要做到百世之后圣人来考察也不会提出质疑。总之，要对社会对民众负责，经得住历史的检验。

57. Every system of moral laws must be based upon the man's own consciousness

【Text】

Every system of moral laws must be based upon the man's own consciousness. It must be verified by the common experience of men. Examined into by comparing it with the teachings of acknowledged great and wise men of the past, there must be no divergence. Applying it to the operations and processes of nature in the physical universe, there must be no contradiction. Confronted with the spiritual powers of the universe a man must be able to maintain it without any doubt. He must be prepared to wait a hundred generations after him for the coming of a man of perfect divine nature to confirm it without any misgiving.

The Universal Order · Chapter XXIX

【Commentary】

Men in authority should proceed with discretion and act in accordance with the universal law. While taking actions, a moral man must take into consideration his own self-cultivation and status, as well as the requests from the general public. He must also draw experience from the history and prepare to wait a hundred generations after him for the coming of a man of perfect divine nature to confirm his actions without any misgivings. In short, he must be responsible for his solutions to social problems, and his measures must stand the test of time.

君子行为天下法

Every thing a moral man does becomes a statute for generations

58. 君子行为天下法

【原文】

是故君子动而世为天下道，行而世为天下法，言而世为天下则。

《中庸·第二十九章》

【释文】

所以君子的举止能世世代代成为天下的先导，行为能世世代代成为天下的法度，言语能世世代代成为天下的准则。

【解析】

在上位的君子行事谨慎是非常重要的，因为他的一举一动、一言一行，都是世人的榜样。

58. Every thing a moral man does becomes a statute for generations

【Text】

Wherefore it is that it is true of the really great moral man, that every act of his life becomes an example for generations; every thing he does becomes a statute for generations, and every word he utters becomes a law for generations.

The Universal Order · Chapter XXIX

【Commentary】

It is critical that the moral man in authority proceeds with discretion, because every act of his life or every word he utters becomes an example for generations.

仲尼祖述尧舜，宪章文武

Confucius taught the truth handed down by
Emperors Yao and Shun; adopted and perfected
the system of moral laws established by the Emperors Wen and Wu

大成殿
萬世師表

59. 仲尼祖述尧舜，宪章文武

【原文】

仲尼祖述尧舜，宪章文武，上律天时，下袭水土。辟如天地之无不持载，无不覆帱。辟如四时之错行，如日月之代明。万物并育而不相害，道并行而不相悖。小德川流，大德敦化。此天地之所以为大也！

《中庸·第三十章》

【释文】

孔子遵循尧、舜的道统，效法文王、武王的典章，上遵循天时，下符合地理。就像天地那样没有什么不承载，没有什么不覆盖。又好像四季的交替运行，日月的轮流照耀。万物一同发育生长而不互相妨害，天地之道同时运行而不互相冲突。小的德行滋润万物如河水一样长流不息，大的德行化生万物使万物敦厚纯朴。这就是天地为什么如此伟大的原因啊！

59. Confucius taught the truth handed down by Emperors Yao and Shun; adopted and perfected the system of moral laws established by the Emperors Wen and Wu

【Text】

Confucius taught the truth originally handed down by the ancient Emperors Yao and Shun, and he adopted and perfected the system of moral laws established by the Emperors Wen and Wu. He showed that they harmonize with the divine order which governs the revolutions of the seasons in the Heaven above and that they fit in with the moral design which is to be seen in physical nature upon the Earth below. These moral laws form one system with the laws by which Heaven and Earth support and contain, overshadow and canopy all things. These moral laws form the same system with the laws by which the seasons succeed each other and the sun and moon appear with the alternations of day and night. It is this same system of laws by which all created things are produced and develop themselves each in its order and system without injuring one another; that the operations of Nature take their course without conflict or confusion; the lesser forces flowing everywhere like river currents, while the great forces of Creation go silently and steadily on. It is this — one system running through all — that makes the Universe so impressively great.

The Universal Order · Chapter XXX

【解析】

孔子继承尧舜禹汤文武周公的传统，以天地为法。天无不覆，地无不载，四季依时轮替，日月昼夜递照，万物并育，诸道兼行。这是天地之诚，也是天地“从容中道”（从容不迫地走在中庸的大道上）的体现。

【Commentary】

Confucius carried on the traditions handed down from Emperors Yao, Shun, Yu, Tang, Wen, Wu and Duke Zhou, and he adopted the universal law. Heaven and Earth support, contain, overshadow and canopy all things. The seasons succeed each other and the sun and the moon appear with the alternations of day and night. All created things develop themselves each in its order and system without injuring one another; the operations of Nature take their course without conflict or confusion. All of these embody the absolute truth of the universe: the moral order.

60. 唯天下至圣，为能聪明睿知

【原文】

唯天下至圣，为能聪明睿知，足以有临也；宽裕温柔，足以有容也；发强刚毅，足以有执也；齐庄中正，足以有敬也；文理密察，足以有别也。

《中庸·第三十一章》

【释文】

只有天下最伟大的圣人，才能如此的聪颖明智，足以居上位而临下民；才能如此的宽容温和，足以包容天下万物；才能如此的奋发刚毅，足以操持决断天下大事；才能如此的庄重恭敬持守中正，足以得到人们的尊敬；才能如此的条理清晰详辨明察，足以分辨是非善恶。

【解析】

至圣之人效法天道之诚，具有最大的聪明智慧，足以统帅民众：他内心宽厚柔顺，足以包容万物；他奋发有为，刚强坚毅，足以决断大事；他严肃庄重，中道而行，足以获得尊敬；他思维缜密，条理清晰，足以分辨是非。由于至圣之人以天为法，“从容中道”，所以达到最高明的境界。

60. Only the man with the most perfect divine moral nature can combine in himself quickness of apprehension, intelligence, insight and understanding

【Text】

It is only the man with the most perfect divine moral nature who is able to combine in himself quickness of apprehension, intelligence, insight, and understanding: qualities necessary for the exercise of command; magnanimity, generosity, benignity and gentleness: qualities necessary for the exercise of patience; originality, energy, strength of character and determination: qualities necessary for the exercise of endurance; dignity, noble seriousness, order and regularity: qualities necessary for the exercise of self-respect; grace, method, delicacy and lucidity: qualities necessary for the exercise of critical judgment."

The Universal Order · Chapter XXXI

【Commentary】

The man with the most perfect divine moral nature abides by the universal law, and maintains the central balance of his moral being, thus he is able to reach the highest excellence.

唯天下至诚，为能经纶天下之大经

Only he in this world who is possessed of absolute truth
can order and adjust the great relations of human society

61. 唯天下至诚，为能经纶天下之大经

【原文】

唯天下至诚，为能经纶天下之大经，立天下之大本，知天地之化育。

《中庸·第三十二章》

【释文】

只有天下达到诚的最高境界的圣人，才能创立天下的常道，才能树立天下的根基，才能执掌天地化育万物的规律。

【解析】

圣人为什么能创立天下的常道，树立天下的根基，执掌天地化育万物的规律呢？他所依靠的是什么呢？他的仁心是那样的诚挚，他的思虑像潭水般幽深，他的大德像苍天一样广阔。他达到了“诚”的最高境界。

61. Only he in this world who is possessed of absolute truth can order and adjust the great relations of human society

【Text】

It is only he in this world who is possessed of absolute truth that can order and adjust the great relations of human society, fix the fundamental principles of morality, and understand the laws of creation of the Universe.

The Universal Order · Chapter XXXII

【Commentary】

He who is possessed of absolute truth can order and adjust the great relations of human society, fix the fundamental principles of morality, and understand the laws of creation of the Universe. Why was he able to do so, and by what means? As a moral man, he has a sincere and honest heart; his thoughts are as profound as the deep pool; his morality is as vast as the heaven. He has reached the state of absolute truth.

62. 君子之道，暗然而日章

【原文】

君子之道，暗然而日章；小人之道，的然而日亡。君子之道，淡而不厌，简而文，温而理，知远之近，知风之自，知微之显，可与入德矣。

《中庸·第三十三章》

【释文】

君子所持之道，深藏不露但日益彰明；小人所持之道，光鲜显露但日益暗淡。君子所持之道，看似平淡但不使人生厌，看似简略但有文采，看似温和但条理井然，知道从近处入手可以达到远方的目标，知道从自身入手可以风化千万的民众，知道从显著入手可以进入精深微妙的境地。这样，就可以进入道德的崇高境界了。

【解析】

君子要保持心性的质朴、平淡、简易、温顺，然后才能深入至圣之人崇高的美德中。

62. The life of the moral man is unobtrusive and yet it grows more and more in significance

【Text】

The life of the moral man is unobtrusive and yet it grows more and more in significance; whereas the life of the vulgar person is ostentatious, but it loses more and more in significance until it becomes nothingness. The life of the moral man is plain, and yet not unattractive; it is simple, and yet full of grace; it is easy, and yet methodical. He knows that accomplishment of great things consists in doing little things well. He knows that great effects are produced by small causes. He knows the evidence and reality of what cannot be perceived by the senses. Thus he is enabled to enter into the world of ideas and morals.

The Universal Order · Chapter XXXIII

【Commentary】

A moral man must develop his inward nature by leading a plain, simple, easy and gentle life. Thus he is enabled to enter into the world of morals.

君子内省不疚

The moral man examines into his own heart and has no cause for self-reproach

63. 君子内省不疚

【原文】

君子内省不疚，无恶于志。君子之所不可及者，其唯人之所不见乎？

《中庸·第三十三章》

【释文】

君子常常自我反省就不会有过失和愧疚，也没有恶念头藏在心志之中。君子的德行之所以为一般人所不及，大概就是在这些不被人看见的地方也能保持恭敬谨慎吧？

【解析】

君子要时常反省自己，还要“慎独”，在人所不见之处也能诚信专一，不背离中道。

63. The moral man examines into his own heart and has no cause for self-reproach

【Text】

Therefore the moral man must examine into his own heart and see that he has no cause for self-reproach, that he has no evil thought in his mind. Wherein the moral man is superior to other men consists even in that which is not seen by men.

The Universal Order · Chapter XXXIII

【Commentary】

The moral man brings introspection frequently to himself, and "watches diligently over his secret thought." He, being true, sincere and single-minded, will not go against the moral order, not even when there are no other people present.

64. 君子不动而敬

【原文】

君子不动而敬，不言而信。

《中庸·第三十三章》

【释文】

君子在没有行动的时候也是恭敬的，在没有言语的时候也是诚信的。

【解析】

君子外在的言行固然重要，但更重要的是内在的恭敬和诚信。

64. The moral man, not doing anything, is serious

【Text】

Therefore the moral man, even when he is not doing anything, is serious; and, even when he does not speak, is truthful.

The Universal Order · Chapter XXXIII

【Commentary】

For a moral man, exterior words and deeds are important. But interior seriousness and truthfulness are even more important.

65. 君子不赏而民劝

【原文】

君子不赏而民劝，不怒而民威于鈇钺。

《中庸·第三十三章》

【释文】

君子不用赏赐民众也会互相劝勉，不用发怒民众也会产生畏惧。

【解析】

君子要以身作则，做到自己不赏赐民众仍受激励，自己不发怒民众也很敬服。

65. The moral man, without the inducement of rewards, is able to make the people good

【Text】

Hence the moral man, without the inducement of rewards, is able to make the people good; and without the show of anger, to awe them into fear more than if he had used the most dreadful instruments of punishment.

The Universal Order · Chapter XXXIII

【Commentary】

A moral man practices what he preaches. He is able to make people feel encouraged and indebted even without rewards; and make people feel awed and respectful even without being furious.

君子笃恭而天下平

The moral man living a life of simple truth and earnestness can bring peace and order in the world

66. 君子笃恭而天下平

【原文】

君子笃恭而天下平。

《中庸·第三十三章》

【释文】

君子笃实恭敬就能使天下太平。

【解析】

君子的表率能收到潜移默化之效，致“治国平天下”之功。子思论“诚”，上承孔子，实际上是论人的信仰和追求，也就是对中庸之道的信仰和追求。只有对崇高信仰的不懈追求，才能达到道德精神的最高境界，从而实现“治国平天下”的宏伟理想。

66. The moral man living a life of simple truth and earnestness can bring peace and order in the world

【Text】

Hence the moral man, by living a life of simple truth and earnestness, alone can help to bring peace and order in the world.

The Universal Order · Chapter XXXIII

【Commentary】

If a moral man can play an exemplary role in society, he will exert a subliminal influence on other people. The "absolute truth" that Zisi discussed here is what human beings are seeking as a religion: the universal moral order. Only the unremitting pursuit of a noble faith could lead a man to the highest state of morality. Thus the mission of "bringing peace and order in the world" can be fulfilled.

予怀明德，不大声以色

I keep in mind the fine moral qualities which make no great noise or show

67. 予怀明德，不大声以色

【原文】

《诗》云：“予怀明德，不大声以色。”子曰：“声色之于以化民，末也。”

《中庸·第三十三章》

【释文】

《诗经·大雅·皇矣》说：“我（上帝）赞赏文王光明的德行，他对待民众从不厉声厉色。”孔子说：“用厉声厉色去教化民众，是舍本而逐末。”

【解析】

君子要效法天地，无声而教，无言而化，达到教化的最高境界。

67. I keep in mind the fine moral qualities which make no great noise or show

【Text】

In the *Book of Songs* it is said: "I keep in mind the fine moral qualities which make no great noise or show." Confucius remarked: "Among the means for the regeneration of mankind, those made with noise and show are of the least importance."

The Universal Order · Chapter XXXIII

【Commentary】

A moral man complies with the universal order; he instructs and influences others without sound or speech, and this is the highest state of the regeneration of mankind.

翻译后记

1910年，清政府赐予十二名因具有“游学专门回国在十年以外者”以“进士及第”的头衔。其中文科的前三名分别为：严复（1854—1921）、辜鸿铭（1856—1928）、伍光健（1867—1943）。众所周知，三人均在欧洲游学多年后回到中国，且皆以翻译上的成就而受到学界瞩目。不同的是，严和伍是向内输入西方近代学理和知识的高产翻译家，而辜鸿铭则是向外输出中国文化与传统的执着代言人。他是第一位通过英语写作和英译儒经而获得国际声誉的中国人。

辜鸿铭于1856年生于马来西亚槟榔屿的一个华人家庭，年少时游学苏格兰、法国及德国，后于1885年左右返回中国。曾任武昌总督府洋文委员、翻译委员，后升任外务部侍郎及上海黄浦江浚浦局总办。清朝灭亡后，他曾任教北京大学。1925年至1927年，他负笈日本讲学，但在1927年4月返回中国后去世，享年72岁。

辜鸿铭在1898年出版英译《论语》，又相继翻译出他非常重视的另两部儒经《中庸》(1906)和《大学》(1915)。辜氏在其著作中反复引用两经中章句的事实说明，他不仅对于这两部经书的内容十分熟稔，理解准确到位，还证明他作为孔门弟子对其笃信不疑的思想与信条进行着亲力亲为的宣讲。但凡有机会，无论大小，辜鸿铭都会毫不例外地鼓励他立志研习国学的外国友人或学生从这两部书开始学起。

由于其在英译儒经方面所作出的贡献，辜鸿铭绝不应被遗忘或低估。他是第一个完成英译《论语》、《中庸》和《大学》的中国人。林语堂对辜的翻译曾作出如下评价：

> 辜氏的翻译是具有创作性的，经典古籍之光通过深邃的哲思得以投射。事实上，他扮演着东西观念电镀匠的角色……他对于儒家经典的翻译甚优，这源自于其对原文的透彻理解。中国古代经典从未有过好的译本。西方汉学家的翻译做得很糟，而中国人自己又疏忽此事。

本书汇集了《大学》和《中庸》的核心章节，英文翻译采用了辜鸿铭先生的版本，根据内容也对译文做出了部分调整。中文选摘及释析由张葆全先生负责完成。英译文的润色调整以及“解析”内容的翻译由吴思远完成。

同时要十分感谢广西师范大学出版社虞劲松老师、施萍老师、王专老师及其他匿名译审老师！没有他们的信任、支持和指导，这本译作是无法完成的。对于译文中仍存在的衍误和不妥之处，译者本人负全部责任。

吴思远

2015 年 11 月 8 日

于美国凤凰城

Postscript

In 1910, the Qing government rewarded few scholars with the degree of *Jinshi* for their achievements in translation. The top three were Yan Fu (1854—1921), Gu Hongming (1856—1928) and Wu Guangjian (1867—1943). Each of them received education in European countries before unanimously returning to China. Yan and Wu were preeminent importers of modern scientific knowledge and scholarship from the West, whereas Gu Hongming was a dedicated exporter and fervent spokesman of Chinese culture and civilization. He was the first Chinese scholar who gained worldwide fame via his English translations of Confucian classics and his writings of social and cultural criticism.

Gu Hongming was born in a Chinese family at Penang in 1956. He studied in Scotland, France and Germany for many years before returning to China around 1885. He then worked for the Qing government by serving successively as secretary, translator, Deputy

Minister of Foreign Affairs Department, and Director of Shanghai Huangpu Conservancy. After the collapse of the Qing regime in 1911, Gu had been teaching in Beijing University for about half a decade until 1920. He stayed almost jobless in his late years and led a semi-exiled life in Japan from 1925 to 1927. He eventually returned to China and died at age 72. Throughout his life, Gu wrote and translated mostly in English and his mastery of a dozen other languages was accomplished with both natural flair and unremitting efforts.

Gu Hongming translated *Lunyu* into English in 1898, and two other classics to which Gu had always attached great importance: *Zhongyong* (1906) and *Daxue* (1915). His repeated quotations from them not only showed his familiarity with the Confucian classics, but also symbolized his practice of promoting what he believed as a disciple of Confucius. Whenever there was a chance, Gu's unexceptionally encouraged his foreign friends and students to start from these two books.

Gu Hongming should never be neglected or underestimated for his translations of Confucian classics. He was the first Chinese scholar who translated *Lunyu*, *Zhongyong* and *Daxue* into English and the latter two into French as well. Lin Yutang regarded Gu's translation efforts as follows:

> It was an act of creative interpretation, a sudden transfusion of light of the old texts through a deep philosophic understanding. He acted, in fact, as the galvanizer of ideas Eastern and Western... His translations of the Confucian books were good because the originals were well understood. Chinese classics had never been

well translated. The Sinologues did a poor job of it, and the Chinese themselves had neglected it.

In this present collection of *Daxue* and *Zhongyong*, we adopted a revised version of Gu Hongming's English translation. The text compiler Mr. Zhang Baoquan provided the Chinese interpretation and commentaries which have been rendered into English by Wu Siyuan.

I would like to express my sincere gratitude to the editors of Guangxi Normal University Press: Mr. Yu Jingsong, Ms. Shi Ping, Ms. Wang Zhuan, and the anonymous proofreaders. This book could not be completed without their trust, support and suggestions. For any errors remain in this book, I take complete responsibility for them.

Wu Siyuan

November 8, 2015

Phoenix, AZ